There are approximately 1 billion Buddhists in the world—all eternally lost. That's sobering! But missionary Mark Durene has identified a powerful strategy to reach them, namely, your prayers. He expresses the need through real stories and gives readers practical tools to help them intercede for a spiritual awakening among the Buddhist people.

Doug Clay
General Superintendent, The General Council of the Assemblies of God (USA)

Seasoned by years of spiritual battle and fruitful ministry, Mark Durene writes compellingly about what it will take to change the spiritual map in the Buddhist world. I found *Change the Map* to be unusually insightful and inspiring.

James Bradford
Lead Pastor, Central Assembly of God, Springfield, Missouri
Former General Secretary, The General Council of the Assemblies of God (USA)

I have had the joy of knowing Mark Durene and following his ministry for a number of years. His strategic thinking, prayer life, integrity, and honesty as a minister and global worker are excellent. I highly recommend *Change the Map*, which vividly describes the nature of sharing the gospel with people who practice Buddhism within the context of understanding the spiritual warfare involved. Mark includes incredible examples of how spiritual battles are fought and won for the Lord Jesus. This book will increase your understanding of the challenges and rewards of reaching a culture and religion with beliefs that are absolutely 180 degrees opposite of Christianity.

Greg Mun
Executive D  *rld Missions (USA)*

D1456818

Change the Map should be standard reading for anyone planning to serve in the Buddhist world. This book allowed me a window into the minds of Buddhists considering the claims of Christ and the incredible spiritual warfare taking place over their lives and souls. Mark's stories are at times humorous and certainly inspirational, causing me to pray more than ever that these never-reached people have a chance to hear.

Jeff Hartensveld
Asia Pacific Regional Director, Assemblies of God World Missions (USA)

In *Change the Map*, Mark Durene does a great job chronicling the everyday challenges missionaries face on the ground when working with Buddhist peoples. This book will give you a fantastic introduction to the spiritual realities of folk Buddhists and help you not only to be burdened to pray for them but to intercede more specifically on key issues.

Alan Johnson
Serving in Thailand since 1986 on behalf of Assemblies of God World Missions (USA)

There may be nothing that holds a bigger place in my heart than reaching the unreached. *Change the Map* is filled with one amazing story after another of how the Holy Spirit overcame incredible obstacles to work in the hearts of Buddhist people. Despite centuries of missionary efforts, the Buddhist world still needs a breakthrough to see Jesus. In this book filled with Mark's adventures, he identifies a common theme that triggers spiritual breakthrough and has the potential to change the spiritual map of the Buddhist world. That excites me! May it be so!

Rob Ketterling
Lead Pastor, River Valley Church
Author, Speed of Unity

CHANGE THE MAP

Impacting the Buddhist World
through Prayer and Action

MARK DURENE

Foreword by James T. Bradford

Printed in the United States of America.

ISBN 978-1-7356545-3-9

*I dedicate this book to my dad, Arthur Durene.
He passed into the arms of the Lord while I was writing
the final chapter. His death accentuated the critical role he
played in preparing me to serve for nearly 30 years as a
missionary to Thailand. He was a solid rock.*

I miss you, Dad.

CONTENTS

FOREWORD

If you are part of Jesus' global mission in any way, then you are a spiritual map-changer. Jesus told His followers to "make disciples of all nations" (Matthew 28:19). In turn He assured them they could be "clothed with power from on high" (Luke 24:49) and promised He would personally be with them "to the end of the age" (Matthew 28:20).

It is to this work of spiritual map-changing that the Lord Jesus will ultimately hold us—the Church—accountable. In his poignant book, *The Cry of the World*, the great missionary-minded pastor, Oswald J. Smith, wrote:

> We should have kept before us our Lord's post-resurrection commands. We should have evangelized the world. Otherwise we have no ground for our existence as a church. There is no reason why we should have churches unless they are reaching out to those who have never heard.[1]

The caution that the Apostle Paul gave us, however, is that there is a "god of this world" who has "blinded the minds of the unbelievers" (2 Corinthians 4:4). In other words, spiritual map-changing will engage us in spiritual battle. Paul underscored that reality in Ephesians 6:12 by reminding us that "our struggle is not against flesh and blood, but against the rulers, against the authorities, against the powers of this dark world and against the spiritual forces of evil in the heavenly realms" (NIV). Yet in spite of demonic resistance, Jesus is still keeping His promise to build His church. The spiritual map of our world is changing!

This shift is happening, in part, through the incredible skill and anointing of missionaries like Mark and Janie

---

1 Oswald J. Smith, *The Cry of the World*, (Great Britain: Purnell and Sons, Ltd., 1959), p. 47.

Durene. Many years ago, I had the privilege of sharing both life and leadership with these remarkably gifted people. I performed their wedding, and Mark eventually succeeded me as the lead pastor of the church that had started out of my student years at the University of Minnesota. Their long-time calling to reach the Buddhist world, however, was finally realized several years later when they moved their young family to Thailand. There they immersed themselves in language, culture, evangelism, leadership mentoring, and church planting.

Now, seasoned by years of spiritual battle and fruitful ministry, Mark writes compellingly about what it will take to change the spiritual map in the Buddhist world. I found *Change the Map* to be unusually insightful and inspiring. His personal journey, his real-life stories, his contextual approach to evangelism, and his gospel understanding touched me deeply. Even more, I was challenged afresh to factor into my own ministry responsibilities the reality of the demonic realm, the place of believing prayer, and the value of strategic intent.

We are each called by Jesus to change the spiritual map in our world. As you read this book, may you feel Mark's deep love for people who Jesus loves and his passion to change the map in the Buddhist world. Whether it be through prevailing prayer or practical partnership, may you hear the Holy Spirit's voice guiding you to personally respond.

James Bradford
Lead Pastor, Central Assembly of God, Springfield, Missouri
Former General Secretary, The General Council of the
Assemblies of God (USA)

PREFACE

I considered writing a book for several years. After nearly three decades as a missionary in Thailand, it still feels like an adventure to me. I love the country, and I love the unique experiences I've had and continue to have. Each experience has taught me something new about myself and about God. My desire to write a book started out as a longing to share those wonderful experiences and lessons with the world. However, it took several years to conjure up the motivation to plunge into a book project. It seemed daunting and time-consuming, and I had doubts about my untested writing skills.

Over the past several months, my motivation to write has been on a steady incline to the point of urgency. The cause of my growing passion is an increasing awareness of the lack of gospel witness to Buddhists and the absence of advocates crying out on their behalf. Followers of Buddhism number between 500 million[2] and 1 billion[3] people, depending on whether various kinds of folk Buddhists are included in the count. Despite these massive numbers—representing beautiful people who are spiritually lost and bound for an eternity separated from God—the frail evangelistic efforts that exist are disheartening. Very little is preached or written or posted concerning the needs of Buddhists, and the Church's efforts to reach them have been lethargic at best.

I hope this book will stir readers' hearts with concern and passion to reach Buddhist people with the gospel message. The book is neither a biography nor a

2 "Buddhists," in *The Future of World Religions: Population Growth Projections, 2010-2050*, Pew Research Center, April 2, 2015, https://www.pewforum.org/2015/04/02/buddhists/.
3 Alex G. Smith, "Counting the Buddhist World Fairly," in *Sharing Jesus Holistically with the Buddhist World*, ed. David Lim and Steve Spaulding (Pasadena, CA: William Carey Library, 2005), 7.

chronological account of my ministry in Thailand but rather a collection of the most impactful and instructional experiences of my missionary career. These experiences highlight the chasm between the Thai spiritual world and God's kingdom. Throughout my ministry in Thailand, I have been surprised over and over by spiritual encounters that caught me unprepared. But every experience demonstrated the reckless love of God and His sovereign wisdom that worked to overcome each obstacle for the purpose of bringing lost people to Himself.

I pray the Holy Spirit will speak through each story and its accompanying spiritual lesson to bring readers to their knees in intercession for Buddhist people and for the missionaries and Christian workers who are actively sharing the gospel with them.

INTRODUCTION
CHANGE THE MAP

In April 2012 Janie and I faced one of the most difficult decisions of our lives. Assemblies of God World Missions (AGWM) Asia Pacific Regional Director Dr. Russ Turney and Executive Director Dr. Greg Mundis flew to Bangkok from the United States and asked me to travel from our base in Chiang Mai to meet them there. No reason was given, so I was nervous. Had I said or done something wrong? Happily, they weren't there to scold me. They informed me that my area director had just accepted a new position in the United States, and they were considering me as his replacement.

The role of area director would mean a radical change of ministry from working with Thai pastors and churches to overseeing some 160 missionaries in five countries. I loved northern Thailand. I loved working with Thai pastors and leaders. I loved preaching and teaching in Thai. I knew I was called to Thailand. I didn't feel called to five countries, and I didn't feel called to lead missionaries.

I told them I was honored by their offer, but I preferred they ask someone else. They reminded me that as a Pentecostal minister I could not accept or decline their offer until after I prayed about it. Touché! They gave Janie and me two weeks to decide.

Back in Chiang Mai, Janie and I talked and prayed
about the opportunity. We had decided long before that
we would live Spirit-led lives, but at that moment it didn't
feel like the Spirit was leading us to change our ministry
focus—especially to that radical degree. As I prayed
and considered the offer, I grew curious about the five
countries I was being asked to serve: Thailand, Vietnam,
Cambodia, Laos, and Myanmar. What were they like? What
were their challenges? Were there good reasons I should
invest there? Were my gifts compatible with their needs?

Thailand was a given. I love Thailand. But as I began to
research the other four countries, the Holy Spirit led me
to a website that shook my world. It featured a CIA map
depicting worldwide Buddhism population percentages.

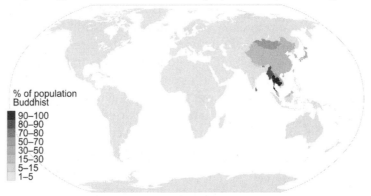

% of population
Buddhist

90–100
80–90
70–80
50–70
30–50
15–30
5–15
1–5

The highest concentrations of Buddhists live in one tiny
corner of the world—the five countries I was being asked
to lead. The dark shading covering the five countries leapt
off my computer screen and into my heart. I felt indignant
and embarrassed that my corner of the world was the
global hotbed of Buddhism. This wasn't right! Jesus died
for Buddhists, and He desires that they would all come
to salvation in Him. Something needed to be done!
Something needed to happen to *change the map*.

Immediately I knew God was calling me to say yes to
the role of Peninsular Asia (PenAsia) area director, and I

knew I had to do something in that role to effect change in the Buddhist world. But what would it take to change the map? I had labored for nearly 20 years in northern Thailand and felt good about my effectiveness. I helped disciple several successful pastors and plant several successful churches. During my ministry, the northern district of the Thailand Assemblies of God had grown from seven or eight churches to 36. But despite my efforts the nation's population was still less than 0.7 percent Evangelical Christians—the same percentage as when I started. Not even 1 percent of the population in the nation has a personal relationship with Jesus!

As I pondered my missionary efforts in Chiang Mai, I began to feel like a failure. If nearly 20 years of ministry failed to make a dent in the statistics, what would it take to effect real change in Thailand and the other four countries I would serve? I didn't know the answer to that question, but I knew it was the challenge I must confront.

My first responsibility as area director began just weeks later. An area-wide retreat was scheduled in Siem Reap, Cambodia, with over 100 missionaries in attendance, and I was their leader. That day I unveiled the new passion the Holy Spirit had placed on my heart: Change The Map.[4]

I presented my map, showing the missionaries that they were working in a powerful Buddhist stronghold. I implored them to own this challenge and commit themselves to doing all they could to change the map. I didn't know exactly what to do with my newfound campaign except to challenge our missionaries to pray with increased focus and intensity and keep working as hard as they could.

A year later I was inspired with a powerful spiritual concept from the Old Testament story of Moses holding up his staff during the Amalekite war with Aaron and Hur at his side (Exodus 17:8–13). Israel was fighting its

4 Since 2017 Change The Map has used a capital "T" in its organizational name.

first military battle after leaving Egypt, and the people were exhausted following their traumatic escape and the harrowing Red Sea experience. The Amalekites took advantage of their vulnerable condition by attacking the stragglers at the end of their long convoy (Deuteronomy 25:17–18). Without hesitation, Moses ordered Joshua to throw together an army in one day and charge into battle against Amalek the next.

The next part of the story is crucial. Moses' staff raised high in intercession before God was more powerful than the Israelites' swords. When Moses raised the staff, Israel prevailed. When he dropped it, they lost ground. I'm sure the soldiers kept fighting hard, but without the support of the raised staff their best effort was not enough to win.

I suddenly knew what we in Peninsular Asia needed more than anything else. I identified personally with the feeling of fighting a battle without the support of an upraised staff. Thousands of missionaries had been battling alongside Thai pastors and Christians, working as hard as they could for nearly 200 years, but they had barely gained any ground. The same is true for missions among every other Buddhist nation and people group in the world, with the possible exception of South Korea.[5] Missionaries and local believers are fighting on the spiritual battleground—brandishing the swords of evangelism and church-planting and disciple-making movements—but they're not winning. They desperately need intercessors to raise the staff of prayer to God on behalf of Buddhists.

BUDDHIST HOLY DAYS

My first step was to call PenAsia missionaries to consistent, focused fasting and prayer every Buddhist holy day. Thai Buddhists do not set aside Fridays, Saturdays, or

5 God did an incredible work in South Korea following World War II, although at the time Buddhism was not strong. It is notable that fervent prayer was the outstanding characteristic of that move of God.

Sundays as their holy days of worship, but instead use the phases of the moon to identify weekly sacred days. Each of the four phases in the lunar cycle—new moon, waxing half-moon, full moon, and waning half-moon—happens roughly seven days apart, and each is designated as a Buddhist holy day. On these days devout Thai Buddhists believe they will receive extra merit for their good deeds, and many make a special effort to visit their local temples to meditate.

In fall 2013 I sent out the first monthly Change The Map prayer guide to my PenAsia missionaries and called them to fast and pray for Buddhists each holy day. I continued sending prayer guides every month with weekly prayer requests. The staff of intercession had begun to rise over the spiritual battlefield in the Buddhist world.

THAT'S NOT FAIR!

Not long after the prayer guides started going out, I happened to be talking to a missionary friend serving in Bangladesh. He told me visions and dreams of Jesus had become normal experiences for the many Muslims converting to Christianity. His next comment floored me. He said he couldn't think of a single convert who had *not* had a vision or dream of Jesus compelling them to turn to Him for salvation.

My reaction surprised me. I blurted out, "That's not fair!" I couldn't help but question why God was giving special treatment to Muslims by appearing to them in visions and dreams while Buddhist hearts seemed to be impervious to the gospel message. God's "normal" evangelistic approach is to use Christians to reach lost people, so why is He taking such a direct approach with Muslims? To be clear, I'm not unhappy that God is blessing the Muslim world. I praise God for miraculously drawing Muslims to Jesus, and I think I know why He is doing it.

When I was attending Bible college, a missionary came to my church to introduce *Jumaa* Prayer Fellowship, an initiative that calls Christians to pray and fast for Muslims every Friday (the Muslim holy day). Over the past 40 years, the list of *Jumaa* Prayer Fellowship intercessors has grown to 60,000 Christians.[6] They are raising the staff of prayer over the spiritual battlefield of the Muslim world, and God is answering their prayers by supernaturally calling Muslims to Himself.

I want that to happen in the Buddhist world! Buddhists need Jesus. Jesus loves them and wants to save them. Buddhists place their hope for salvation upon their personal ability to navigate the Noble Eightfold Path of self-effort to attain enlightenment. Buddhists teach that they cannot rely on someone or something else to achieve this goal; they must do it on their own. Today up to 1 billion Buddhists throughout the world are meditating, making merit, spinning prayer wheels, prostrating, chanting, lighting incense, and striving in a myriad of other ways to save themselves. It is futility, "for by works of the law no human being will be justified in his sight" (Romans 3:20).

I have become painfully aware that 160 prayerful, hardworking missionaries are not powerful enough to change the map in the Buddhist world! You, the people of God, must hold high the staff of intercession that brings spiritual victory. I am convinced that when tens of thousands of Christians begin to intercede on behalf of Buddhists, God will sovereignly break down the many barriers that blind their spiritual eyes to who He is and how much He loves them. Intercessors are the key to changing the map of the Buddhist world. I now know what the focus of the rest of my life must be: raising up an army of intercessors to pray for Buddhists.

---

6 Pray | Global Initiative: Reaching Muslim Peoples. https://www.reachingmuslimpeoples.com/get-involved. Accessed 1/13/2021.

SPIRITUAL INSIGHTS & PRAYERS

Missiologists say there are approximately 1 billion Buddhists in the world. They are eternally lost without Jesus' saving grace. Missionaries work hard, but they cannot win the Buddhist world to Jesus alone. Just as Moses' staff ensured Israel's triumph over the Amalekites, the staff of intercession is our key to victory. You hold the staff. Your prayers are needed to Change The Map.

PRAY FOR BUDDHISTS

I pray for the 1 billion Buddhists in the world who need You as Savior and Lord. Please reveal Yourself to them, communicate Your love to them, open their minds to Your truth, and open their hearts to receive You.

PRAY FOR MISSIONARIES

I lift up the staff of intercession on behalf of missionaries and Christian workers living and ministering in the Buddhist world. Cover them with anointing, fill them with faith and boldness, and let Your provision and protection rest on them and their families.

PRAY FOR YOURSELF

Through the battles in my life, I pray You will give me faith and courage to place my trust in the staff more than the sword. Burden my heart to pray for Buddhists with the love and concern You have for them. Use me as part of the army of intercessors who will change the map for Your sake.

* See Appendix B for a compiled list of spiritual insights and prayers.

CHAPTER ONE

THE DOME

In early February 1994, my wife Janie and I moved our family from the sub-zero temperatures of Minnesota to the sweltering climate of Chiang Mai, Thailand. We quickly found out acclimating ourselves to the weather was easy compared to the cultural and spiritual adjustments in store for us. In fact, we were about to encounter challenges far beyond the *adjustment* category. Thailand would soon change our entire worldview.

Our family had talked about moving to Thailand for several years, but actually making the move was a big deal. Our kids were 12, 10, and 5 years old, and although they were excited about the big adventure, they were sad to leave friends and extended family. The older two were nervous about attending a new school and finding friends. Janie and I knew we were following God's clear, specific call to Thailand, but we were feeling the pressure of settling our family in this strange place.

After we landed in Bangkok, we spent several days adjusting to the 12-hour time difference and getting to know some of the local missionaries before continuing to our destination city. Veteran missionary Alan Johnson accompanied us on the short flight to Chiang Mai, and another veteran missionary family, the Gutels, drove up from Bangkok in a Toyota Corolla they left with us until we could buy our own car. We would have been lost without their guidance during those early days. In just over a week, they helped us find a house to rent, register our kids at Chiang Mai International School, enroll in Thai language school, and arrange dozens of other details.

To our surprise, renting a house in Chiang Mai turned out to be a spiritual adventure. It taught us the first of many spiritual lessons that could only be learned while living and ministering among people who hold a vastly different worldview from ours. My theology was both stretched and enriched by Thai culture, which is much closer to Jesus' Eastern context than our American culture is.

Many experiences challenged what I had been taught in my intercultural studies program at North Central University. Others helped me better understand Jesus' parables and sermons. Ultimately, every experience helped me to better know and understand the Creator of the universe.

HOUSE HUNTING

The Gutels came up with a list of houses available around town, and we started our search. We were reasonably happy with all our choices, especially since the books we had read about Thailand suggested we might be staying in a wooden house on stilts. All the Chiang Mai houses we looked at were made of stucco with either tile or parquet flooring. We could certainly live with that.

But one thing bothered us: A spirit house stood in the corner of every front yard except one. Spirit houses look like dollhouses on posts, and we learned their purpose was to host the spirit owners of each property. Thai Buddhists believe individual spirits own each piece of property and intervene in the occupants' lives. They believe these spirits provide good fortune if treated well and bad fortune if mistreated. Most households assign a family member, usually the grandmother, to mind the spirit house daily by providing food, drink, and incense. The spirit never actually eats or drinks, of course, but is believed to be placated by the fragrance of the offering.

The house we liked best was different from the others. It was the right size, in the right place, at the right price. We wanted that house, but there were some challenges. Although no spirit house stood outside, the property was much spookier than the others because of what was *inside*.

A huge room on the second level served as a worship chamber. A long table flanked one wall, and it was covered with idols, burning candles, and smoking incense. Amid the idols stood a photograph of a long-bearded, long-haired Indian guru. When I saw it, I remembered having spotted a photo of the same person on the living room wall downstairs. On a chair next to the table, a life-sized photo depicted the Indian guru from his waist up. A pair of pants lay on the chair with the legs draped to meet a pair of sandals on the floor, creating the illusion of the guru sitting there looking at us. A small kneeling pillow lay a few feet in front of the chair, and there were wax drippings on the floor in front of it. To this day, I don't know what the homeowner was doing with candles while she knelt in front of the guru's photograph, but it was certainly something spiritual.

Smiling broadly, the landlady told us she sought wisdom from this guru every day, and he responded by giving her advice. She assured us she would remove all her idols if we decided to rent her house.

The presence of spiritual darkness filled that house. We all sensed it, but for some reason, our son Jeris felt it most strongly. During our tour, he refused to go in the house. He felt sick to his stomach and sat on the steps outside.

Our intercessors serve a critical role as we follow the guiding hand of Jesus. Missionaries cannot accomplish God's work in God's power without the support of prayer partners.

The spiritual presence throughout the house made it difficult for the rest of us to explore freely, but still, it was the right size, in the right place, at the right price.

We returned to our guest house that evening to try to decide together which house we should rent, weighing the advantages and disadvantages of the three or four we liked best. Both Janie and I liked the guru house, but we were deeply concerned about the spiritual presence there. It seemed like a dangerous place for our family. How could we bring our young children into an environment like that? What effects would it have on them? Would it cause fear or sickness? Would it affect their relationships with God? Would it hinder our ministry?

Yet all the other homes had spirit houses in the front yard. Almost 95 percent of Thais are Buddhists at least nominally,[7] and most believe in property spirits. Likely all the houses we were considering were under the same spiritual influence. There were no safe options!

Janie and I gathered our family in a circle in the guest house living room and prayed. We asked the Lord for

7 "Thailand," *The World Factbook*, Central Intelligence Agency, updated March 9, 2021, https://www.cia.gov/the-world-factbook/countries/thailand /#people-and-society.

wisdom and guidance to help us with a decision we felt completely unprepared to make. Just a few minutes into the prayer something happened that I wish would happen every time I pray. The Holy Spirit dropped a Scripture into my mind–a clear, commanding word that answered our prayer and canceled our fears. "Greater is he that is in you, than he that is in the world" (1 John 4:4, KJV).

Immediately I stopped and shared the verse with my family, and it became a powerful point of faith in our lives from that moment on. Our decision seemed dangerous. We were considering moving into a house with a demonic presence, inhabited by the "ruler of this world" (John 16:11), or at least his representative. I envisioned us entering an atmosphere inhabited by a dark, demonic enemy force dedicated to destroying God's work in us, who did not want us in Thailand and specifically in that house. But God's promise in that moment was clear. The Holy Spirit within us was greater than the presence of darkness in that guru house. This was our new home.

THE PRAYER FACTOR

Missionaries often tell stories of God's miraculous intervention in their daily lives. I'm sure there are many reasons miracles seem to happen more frequently on the mission field, but I believe prayer support is the most obvious explanation.

We didn't experience miracles all the time, but that day when we heard the voice of the Holy Spirit directing us to rent the guru house, I felt something different. God was directing our lives in a special way that was more clear than anything we experienced during our ministry in Minnesota. I now believe this was a direct result of people actively praying for us. During our 18 months of fundraising, we not only raised monthly financial pledges but also prayer pledges. We went to Thailand with a list of over 600 people who had promised to pray for our family and ministry during our four-year term. Our intercessors serve a critical role as we follow the guiding hand of Jesus. Missionaries cannot accomplish God's work in God's power without the support of prayer partners.

I believe the moment we knelt in prayer to ask for God's direction in choosing a house, someone was praying for us. We grew to rely on those prayers, frequently finding ourselves in need of divine intervention for critical decision-making, words of wisdom, miracles, authority over demonic powers, and many other situations requiring more than human capabilities. During those moments we sensed God's special favor on us as our supporters prayed for us. Prayers for missionaries are necessary, and they are powerful.

HOUSEWARMING

Our only connection in Chiang Mai was a small Assemblies of God church that had been planted three years earlier. Before we moved into the guru house, the Gutels invited the pastor to pray over it. To our surprise, the entire church turned up for a housewarming "party," although we quickly discovered a housewarming in Thailand is less a party than a full-fledged prayer meeting.

Early one evening 30-some people from the church crowded into the large room on the second floor that had housed the guru worship chamber. Through a translator I welcomed them, introduced my family, and described in detail what the room used to look like with all its idols and candle drippings. No one seemed surprised.

The pastor said a few things in Thai, and everyone prayed loudly and enthusiastically for a short time. Suddenly they all got up, still praying, and began looking carefully through every room in the house as if they were searching for something. Not understanding the language or customs, my family and I felt more than a little uncomfortable with this, but only for a few moments.

Soon a young man started shouting. He was leaning out of our second-floor window, pulling on a piece of white string, which we discovered was wrapped around the entire house. A few believers cut it down, and we later learned that when Buddhist monks are invited to bless people's houses, the ceremony involves tying a string around the house to repel evil spirits. The Thai Christians recognized the spiritual power of the string was certainly not from God and needed to be removed.

Then we heard another shout from downstairs. I got to the bottom of the stairs just in time to see someone tear a wooden snake dragon carving off the wall where it had been glued, leaving a very noticeable mark. I wondered how we would explain it to the landlord. Someone else was taking embossed silver bowls off a shelf in the living room, while others were removing candles that lined the perimeter fence.

Somkiet, the best English speaker in the church, asked, "Is it okay with you if they light a fire in your front yard?"

"I guess so," I answered. In a moment all the items they collected—except the silver bowls and the snake dragons—were on fire.

In essence, the church performed a spiritual housecleaning for us that evening. Far better than I, they knew what they were praying for and how to do so. They identified the religious objects and understood the importance of removing and destroying them. They spiritually prepared the way for our family to move into this dark place, illuminating it with the presence of the Holy Spirit, which is greater than any other spiritual force in the world.

GOD'S PRESENCE IN OUR HOUSE

I clearly remember our family's first few nights in the guru house. I felt wary about the possibility of spiritual attack. My two oldest kids, Krista and Jeris, slept in bedrooms on the first floor, while the rest of us slept on the second floor. When I put the kids to bed, I prayed for them as I always did, but these nights I prayed with far more intensity than usual. I tried not to scare them as I prayed, but inwardly I was asking God to protect them from fear, bad dreams, and demonic attack. When I closed their doors, I placed my hands on their doorframes and asked God to station angels there. For the first several nights, I walked through the house before going to bed and prayed for God's presence to fill each room and remove all traces of other spirits. My prayer life was stronger during the first weeks in that house than ever before.

In fact, my morning devotions were powerful during those days as well. Diving into spiritually dark waters drove me to greater reliance on God. Spiritual opposition—or opposition of any kind—motivates us to pursue greater intimacy with God. When we respond to crisis by drawing closer to God and increasing in faith rather than cringing in fear, we foil the plans formed against us and bring good out of bad. Joseph understood this when he told his brothers, "You meant evil against me, but God meant it for good" (Genesis 50:20).

GOD'S PRESENCE THICKENS

Early in my pastoral ministry in Minneapolis, I attended a Marvin Gorman pastors' school in Baton Rouge, Louisiana. At the time Gorman was leading a successful church of thousands. His ministry was marked by miracles, healings, words of knowledge, and other signs and wonders. But it wasn't always that way. During the pastors' school, he recounted a powerful turning point early in his ministry career. His church had been doing well, but it was not experiencing the presence and power of God that he longed for. He prayed for signs and wonders, but none came. He grew more and more desperate, until one day he decided he would pray at least an hour a day, asking God to work through him in miraculous ways.

Every day Gorman rose early to pray. He lay behind the living room sofa to muffle the sounds of his prayers and avoid waking up his family. That spot on the floor became his meeting place with God. Even though his cries didn't seem to make a difference in his ministry, he didn't stop praying. After six years Gorman noticed the place on the carpet where his tears fell had begun to sprout mold.

One Sunday morning after his sermon, Gorman invited people to line up for prayer along the altar. As he was reaching out to pray for the first person in line, that person fell backwards on the floor before Gorman's hand made contact, and they were instantly healed. Gorman was shocked. This had not happened before. He moved to the second person in line. They fell in the same way. As he moved down the line, every person fell backwards and was touched in some miraculous way. From that day on, Gorman's ministry was marked by signs and wonders, and he credited it largely to six years of faithfully crying out to God to use him for God's glory.

During the pastors' school, I saw several miracles happen before my eyes. The experience made such a powerful impression on me that I promised God I would pray daily that He would use me for His glory. That started a lifetime habit of morning devotions that continues to this day.

During the early days in the guru house, despite being highly motivated to pray, I often felt uneasy in my spirit and distanced from God. But as I remained faithful in daily prayer, it became easier and easier to hear His voice. I experienced an ever-increasing sense of God's presence in that house, and it eventually became a sanctuary of ministry. Several young believers lived with our family for months at a time as we discipled them. Multiple Bible study groups and evangelistic outreaches took place in that house. Several young people were saved there, and others were called into full-time ministry.

No matter how dark a home, workplace, or community's spiritual history may be, it cannot overcome the presence of God living in us. *Greater is He that is in us than he that is in the world!* But we must be faithful to pursue intimacy with God every day. The closer we are to God, the stronger His presence is within us. The same is true about our home: The more time we spend with God there, the more we—and other people—sense His presence.

I encourage you to frequently and faithfully spend time with God in your home. Read the Word. Pray. Worship. Commune with God. The more you do it, the easier it will be to commune with Him and sense His presence.

DOME OF PROTECTION

After we'd been living in Thailand about a year, Janie and I were returning home one evening from an outreach at Chiang Mai University. We were discouraged about something that had happened that day, and Janie lamented that it seemed like every time we took a step forward in ministry, Satan violently pushed us backward. Suddenly my attention was drawn to the spirit houses in front of nearly all the homes and businesses we drove by. It felt like the whole city was dedicated to demonic spirits, and they were lining the streets to watch us drive past. For a moment I felt exposed and vulnerable. Could we be in danger living in such a dark place?

In that vulnerable moment, the words of 1 John 4:4 came back to me. *Greater is He that is in us than he that is in the world.* Someone must have been praying for us at that moment, because I immediately envisioned a transparent dome of protection covering Janie and me as we drove down the street. It did not matter how dark the environment around us was, the Almighty Creator God was living in us, and demonic forces could not penetrate that dome. It was a revelation that encouraged me frequently throughout my ministry in Thailand, and it has proven true again and again over the nearly 30 years we have spent in Thailand. As long as I submit to Him daily, I am living under God's dome of protection, and the spiritual forces of darkness cannot overcome me.

As I remained faithful in daily prayer, it became easier and easier to hear His voice. I experienced an ever-increasing sense of God's presence in that house, and it eventually became a sanctuary of ministry.

You may not be living in the demonic darkness of Thailand, but there is a powerful word of encouragement for all God's people in this *dome* principle. Daniel experienced it when he was loathed, plotted against, and thrown into a den of lions. The lions were dangerous, powerful, and hungry, but God placed a dome of protection around him, sending an angel to shut the lions' mouths (Daniel 6:22). Notice God did not remove Daniel from his hostile environment but rather protected him within it.

The psalmist David wrote, "Even though I walk through the valley of the shadow of death, I will fear no evil, for you are with me.… You prepare a table before me in the presence of my enemies" (Psalm 23:4-5). God did not remove David from the valley of the shadow of death or the presence of his enemies, but He was with him, protecting him inside that environment. When I read verse 4, I envision a lone sheep striding confidently through a valley filled with predators and pitfalls, covered by a dome of protection. Verse 5 conjures a picture of someone seated at a table directly across from threatening enemies, protected under a transparent dome and completely at peace.

Be encouraged. If God can protect Daniel in a lions' den, guard a lone sheep in a valley of death, and preserve our family in a hostile spiritual environment, He can cover you with His dome of protection wherever you are today.

SPIRITUAL INSIGHTS & PRAYERS

When you follow God's leading to the best of your ability—no matter where you live, work, or travel—you dwell under the dome of God's protection. If God protected me and my family through the intense spiritual darkness of the guru house, He will protect you through your trials. When spiritual forces attack from every side, you can be confident that His mighty power living inside you is greater than the power of evil that surrounds you on the outside.

PRAY FOR BUDDHISTS

I pray for Buddhist-background believers throughout the world who are living in atmospheres of pervasive spiritual darkness. God, please cover them with a dome of spiritual protection. Instead of giving in to fear or succumbing to the evil that surrounds them, may they be strong and courageous under Your wings (Psalm 91).

PRAY FOR MISSIONARIES

Holy Spirit, please cover missionaries and Christian workers with Your dome of protection wherever they are. I pray 1 John 4:4 over them.

PRAY FOR YOURSELF

Wherever I go and whatever I do, let the indwelling presence of the Holy Spirit surround and protect me. According to Psalm 91, I place my trust in You.

CHAPTER TWO
PROPERTY SPIRITS

One morning I received a call from Sam and Lyn, a couple who attended the small church we were serving in Chiang Mai. They were building a home on a piece of property they had just purchased. The contractor prepared the landscape and poured the foundation for the cement columns of the house, but there was a problem: He told Sam it was time for the column-blessing ceremony.

This ceremony involved asking (and paying for) the local Buddhist monks to bless the construction project. More than that, it meant asking permission of the property's spirit-owner to erect a house on its land. The monks would discern the kind of offering this spirit demanded and how much it would cost, and our friends would be obligated to pay that amount, plus the monks' ceremonial fees. The monks would present the offering to the spirit-owner and honor the spirit through chanting, meditating, lighting incense, and performing other ceremonial activities. When they sensed the spirit-owner was satisfied, they would bless the project.

Sam and Lyn told the contractor they were Christians and did not want to do the ceremony, and an argument ensued. The contractor said this was an important ritual, and it must be done. Sam refused. Finally the contractor said he would not continue with the building, and none of his employees would be allowed to come to work, until the ceremony took place. He explained that the project would be a disaster if the spirit-owner were not appeased. Accidents would happen. Problems would plague them. Money would be lost. From his perspective, no one in their right mind would consider building on a piece of property without performing this ceremony.

An odd idea occurred to Sam. He asked the contractor if he would consent to having a Christian monk do the ceremony. After some thought, the contractor agreed. He said if the Christian monk would obtain permission and blessing from the spirit-owner to build on the property, then he and his workers would come back to finish the house.

That is why Sam and Lyn called me that morning. I was their Christian monk! I was not familiar with the column-blessing ceremony, to put it mildly. It had not been covered in my pastoral theology classes at North Central University. But I told them I would do it.

Janie and I went to our knees in prayer. There were many occasions in Thailand when we did not know what to do. We relied on the Holy Spirit to show us what to say and do, and as the years passed, we developed a dependence not only on the Holy Spirit but on those who were praying for us. We often sensed in our spirits that someone was praying for us during those critical moments. Time and time again, the Holy Spirit showed us what to do when we faced things we were not—and could not be—prepared for. This was one of those occasions.

After praying together, we sensed the Holy Spirit leading us to bring communion elements with us to the construction site. When we arrived, the workers were already gone, so it was just Sam, Lyn, Janie, and me. We joined hands and prayed, asking God for guidance. Then we walked around the perimeter of the property, praying and singing worship songs. We commanded demonic spirits to leave and invited the Holy Spirit to make His residence there.

As we prayed and walked, a troublesome thought came to my mind. For centuries, maybe even millennia, this property had been committed to a spirit-owner. Faithful (possibly daily) sacrifices of food, incense, and meditation had been offered, and it seemed plausible that a demonic spirit, maybe the same one for centuries, had accepted the sacrifices and was present. I certainly felt it was present. I recalled reading books that referenced territorial spirits. When I read them, I was a bit skeptical, wondering if territorial spirits were biblical or how one could ascertain that a demonic spirit possessed a particular territory.

But as we walked and prayed and I mulled over the new ideas in my mind, I suspected that if a demonic spirit were present, it considered this piece of land to be its property and considered us a threat. Could we expect to remove such a spirit with a prayer walk once or twice around the lot? And once it was cast out, could we expect it to stay out? I didn't know the answers, but the four of us were motivated to pray energetically and emphatically.

After our prayer walk, we brought our communion elements to the main column of the house. We prepared the grape juice and bread and I read the traditional passage in 1 Corinthians 11. We prayed, thanking Jesus for His atoning work on the cross. In that spiritual context, I suddenly became aware of a powerful message Paul declared in Colossians 2:15: "[On the cross, Jesus] disarmed the rulers and authorities and put them to open shame, by triumphing over them in him." Jesus' atoning work included victory over the spiritual powers of darkness! I felt emboldened.

We poured the extra grape juice on the ground around the main column, dedicated the property to Jesus, and prayed for protection on the contractor and construction workers, God's favor on the building project, and blessings on Sam and Lyn.

During the weeks that followed, I worried a bit about the project and the builders. I suppose that does not say much for my faith, but in fairness, I did not yet have a firm understanding of biblical principles concerning property spirits or the rights and privileges of believers.

Janie and I continued to pray for the project, and the construction went smoothly. We were excited to be invited back to conduct the spiritual housewarming when the building was completed. That was a ceremony we knew something about!

Please don't misunderstand me. Our prayer walk and communion ceremony were not secret patterns for removing property spirits from a home or piece of land. It was something the Holy Spirit led us to do on that occasion. It was one of the many lessons I learned about the existence and nature of demonic spirits. Over the years those experiences helped me develop biblical teachings about demons and how they might interact with us.

I realize writing about demons and property spirits will raise skepticism in the minds of some readers. In fact, I would have been skeptical as a pastor in Minneapolis a few years earlier. It is typically uncomfortable to discuss the subject of demons with American Christians. But most Thai people accept the concept that property spirits are real, inhabiting land, objects, people, and nature all around them. Living in Thailand presented many occasions to witness overt spiritual activity to the point that my worldview regarding the supernatural began to change. I went to the Scriptures to understand what was happening in the spiritual world around me, and several of those studies are reflected in this book.

THE LATENT POWER OF THE SPIRIT

When I was a teenager, I loved to read. I'm embarrassed to admit I read less now than I did then. One Wednesday night I picked out a small book in the church library. Written by a Chinese pastor, it explained paranormal activity from his Eastern theological perspective. Growing up in a Buddhist environment, he had strong opinions about spirits and mystical things. I was skeptical, to put it mildly.

I never forgot that strange book. It depicted Adam as a superhero (before sin entered the world in Genesis 3) with an incredible mental capacity to name all the animals and birds and remember their names (2:19-20). His strength was so great that he tended the Garden of Eden and gathered food for himself without even sweating (3:19). After the fall Adam lost his special powers, but the Chinese author believed Adam's pre-fall superpowers still reside within the human soul in a latent form. He believed this explains the paranormal activity common throughout Asia. Satan draws upon the latent power of the soul, he explained, enabling people to do magic, tell fortunes, perform healings, meditate, and experience all kinds of paranormal phenomena.

I remain skeptical of the author's conclusions, although it's a thought-provoking concept. Living in Thailand for nearly 30 years has shifted my worldview and theological perspective in an easterly direction. I only bring it up because I have come to believe in the existence of a different latent power, namely the latent power of the *spirit*. I believe God endued the human spirit with special and potentially dangerous power and privilege.

What is the human spirit? God created us in His image and likeness, and "God is spirit" (John 4:24). What does that look like? For one thing, God can appear in various forms. He appeared in a fiery bush (Exodus 3:1-17), in a pillar of fire and a pillar of cloud (13:21), showing only His back (33:23), as a loud voice in thick darkness (Deuteronomy 5:22), and as a low whisper (1 Kings 19:12). Through much of Old Testament history, God's presence resided in the ark of the covenant, specifically between the outstretched wings of the two cherubim on its cover (Exodus 25:22). If that seems like a small space for the Almighty Creator, it *is*. Solomon acknowledged that God is too big to be contained in the highest heavens—say nothing about a small space in the Temple (1 Kings 8:27). God is spirit, which means He is not limited to the physical laws of our universe.

The primary function of the human spirit is to interact with God. He designed us to communicate with Him spirit-to-spirit. The Scriptures teach us the nature of the human spirit includes immortality, which differs from God's eternal nature. Where and when a human spirit begins is an interesting study, but I will resist the temptation to address it here. Regardless of the details of its origin, the human spirit within you right now is *powerful*.

IDOLS EVERYWHERE

To illustrate the power of the human spirit, let's back up a bit to set the scene. Thailand is a spiritual place with idols everywhere. Most Buddhist temples house thousands of idols, and in the central worship building of the temple (called the *boht*) there is usually one large golden Buddha idol situated in the center of the back wall. It is surrounded by dozens of other smaller idols, and hundreds more—depicting Buddha, former monks, or demonic figures—sit all around the temple grounds. Most temples also have a stockpile of idols to sell to visitors.

Outside of Buddhist temples, idols stand in cars, homes, restaurants, businesses, public parks, government buildings, town squares, and even remote places like mountaintops and caves. Thai people believe idols have power to hear and answer prayer. Students crowd their university's main shrine before finals. People who need financial help flock to temples. Sick people travel long distances to visit idols said to have the most healing power.

It is not uncommon to hear testimonials of prayers answered by idols. Thai people are not surprised or even skeptical when they hear stories of miracles resulting from prayer before idols. As Christians, how do we respond to such testimonials? Does supernatural power exist in idols? Let's take a closer look at what the Bible says.

A BIBLICAL PERSPECTIVE ON IDOLS

The spiritual culture in biblical times was similar to Thailand's. Idols, images, and idolatry are referred to at least 228 times in the Old and New Testaments. Over and over, the people of God are warned to stay away from idols. The significance of the idol problem in Old Testament times was accentuated by the second of the Ten Commandments: "You shall not make for yourself a carved image" (Exodus 20:4).

The prophet Isaiah scoffed at idols and idol makers. One can almost hear the disdain in his words as he poked fun at those who made and worshiped idols:

> *All who fashion idols are nothing, and the things they delight in do not profit.... He cuts down cedars, or he chooses a cypress tree or an oak and lets it grow strong among the trees of the forest. He plants a cedar and the rain nourishes it. Then it becomes fuel for a man. He takes a part of it and warms himself; he kindles a fire and bakes bread. Also he makes a god and worships it; he makes it an idol and falls down before it. Half of it he burns in the fire. Over the half he eats meat; he roasts it and is satisfied. Also he warms himself and says, "Aha, I am warm, I have seen the fire!" And the rest of it he makes into a god, his idol, and falls down to it and worships it. He prays to it and says, "Deliver me, for you are my god!" (Isaiah 44:9,14-17)*

Isaiah strongly made the point that idols are natural, not supernatural. They are simply metal (verse 10) or wood, and their makers are mere humans who get hungry, weak, thirsty, and cold (verses 11–15). Isaiah mocked idol worshipers as deluded, because they prostrate themselves in worship before a powerless formation of lifeless material. And Isaiah was not the only one making these claims. A multitude of Scriptures depict idols as powerless and unable to see, speak, or respond.

Why did God warn His people so often and so strongly against idol worship? Paul addressed this question in 1 Corinthians 10, where he warned Christians against idolatry and cautioned them about eating food that had been offered to idols. He gave several reasons for avoiding it in subsequent verses, but he began by addressing the nature of idols.

> *What do I imply then? That food offered to idols is anything, or that an idol is anything? No, I imply that what pagans sacrifice they offer to demons and not to God. I do not want you to be participants with demons. You cannot drink the cup of the Lord and the cup of demons. You cannot partake of the table of the Lord and the table of demons. (1 Corinthians 10:19–21)*

In verse 19, Paul asked the question, Is an idol anything? In other words, "Is there anything inherently powerful, significant, or dangerous in the idol itself?" He answered his own question in verse 20: *No.* There is nothing significant in the idol itself. Paul seemed to be using Isaiah's argument to make the point that idols are simply pieces of inanimate material: wood, metal, or stone. *Inanimate* means "not alive." So if idols are not significant or alive, why do they get so much attention in the Bible? Why do so many Scriptures—from Exodus to the epistles—forbid idols?

Paul's next statement is incredibly insightful. In verse 20 Paul wrote that sacrifices being offered to idols are in actuality being offered to *demons*. As Corinthian people brought their food to the temple idol to appease it and obtain blessings, they were not just placing it before an idol, but a demon. Paul claims demons are connected with, or perhaps attached to, the idols to which the Corinthians were presenting their food. But how did demons get attached to lifeless, powerless idols?

Paul was not unfamiliar with demons. In Philippi he had commanded a demon to come out of a servant girl (Acts 16:16–18). In Ephesus demons came out of people who came in contact with handkerchiefs and aprons he had touched (Acts 19:12). Exorcism was a normal part of his ministry to the point that seven sons of the high priest Sceva tried to copy him and failed in a dramatic, embarrassing fiasco (verses 13–17). In other Scriptures Paul referred to spiritual warfare (2 Corinthians 10:3–6), the hierarchy of the spiritual realm (Ephesians 6:11–20), and "the evil one" (2 Thessalonians 3:3).

It is not uncommon to see a pickup truck on a Thailand highway with a large Buddha idol in the back. More than likely the idol was purchased by a Thai citizen who wanted to obtain special merit by donating it to his favorite temple. Whenever I follow one of these idol-carrying pickups down the road, I wonder if that idol is simply an inanimate piece of metal or if there is a demon attached to it. Paul's demonology said the Corinthians were sacrificing food to demons, but how and when does an inanimate piece of metal contract a demon?

The answer is *spiritual worship*. The human spirit has power to move the spiritual realm through worship.

Worship has many meanings. Merriam-Webster defines it this way: "to honor or show reverence for as a divine being or supernatural power...adore, deify, glorify, revere, reverence, and venerate." Many of us think of it as the worship time before the sermon at church on Sunday morning. For our purposes I will define it as "submitting oneself to or placing oneself under the power of someone or something else."

The most common word for *worship* in the New Testament is the Greek word *proskuneo* (προσκυνεω), from which we derive *prostrate*. It conveys an attitude of reverence, bowing down, or even lying facedown in a display of veneration and submission. When we worship God, we place ourselves *under* His power, His authority, His love, His grace, and His will for our lives. At the same time, we place Him *above* us as our leader, owner, protector, guide, and Savior.

In Thailand idol worship is public. It is common to see people fall to their knees with their hands clasped before idols in temples and other public places. Many worshipers touch their foreheads to the floor three times, indicating submission and respect for Buddha, his teachings, and the monks.

When people worship anything but God, they submit themselves to something other than God and invite or even *invoke* a demonic presence. *Worship* attaches demons to idols. I will defend this radical claim in the next chapter.

SPIRITUAL INSIGHTS & PRAYERS

Idols are powerless until people worship them. This principle is true whether the idol is a figurine, a person, or even a concept. When people worship anything or anyone besides God, they expose themselves to the risk of demonic activity. Thai Buddhists and the majority of Eastern Buddhists believe idols and spirits are real and powerful. They worship them openly, resulting in an atmosphere charged with spiritual activity. Our prayers are needed to release people from the control of demons and open their spiritual ears to hear the voice of the Holy Spirit calling to them through the darkness.

PRAY FOR BUDDHISTS

I pray for Buddhists throughout the world who live in atmospheres of intense spiritual darkness. May their eyes be drawn to the light. May their ears be open to the truth. May their minds comprehend the gospel. May their spirits be receptive to Jesus' saving power so they can say, "He has delivered us from the domain of darkness and transferred us to the kingdom of his beloved Son" (Colossians 1:13).

PRAY FOR MISSIONARIES

I pray for strength for missionaries and Christian workers who are ministering in spiritually dark places. I prayerfully support them in spiritual warfare, according to Ephesians 6:10-12.

PRAY FOR YOURSELF

I pray that I would never worship anything besides You, according to Exodus 20:3. You are the Lord of my life, my thoughts, my decisions, my possessions, my relationships, my past, my present, and my future.

CHAPTER THREE

THE SECRET POWER OF WORSHIP

One of the many challenges in discipling new Thai believers is conveying the critical necessity of renouncing the many "gods" in their lives.

I love Thai people and Thai culture in general. Most Thai people are polite, gracious, kind, affirming, and agreeable. Although the vast majority are Buddhist, they feel no obligation to explain or defend their religion. Buddhism is not something they choose but something they are born into, and many believe it is impossible not to be Buddhist. That makes it extremely challenging for them to become Christ-followers, but strangely enough, it makes it easy to talk to them about Christianity. The discussion is not threatening to their Buddhism but is merely a cross-cultural curiosity.

In all my years in Thailand, I can't recall ever being rejected when I offered to pray for a Thai person. During the COVID-19 crisis, it was easy to obtain permission to pray for people who were nervous about contracting the virus. Thais are receptive to spiritual blessing, regardless of the spirit giving it. They believe there are many kinds of spirits, each with their own specialty and level of power, and each spirit has the potential to either bless or curse them. If one is nice to a given spirit, it will likely provide blessings; if one is disrespectful to that same spirit, it will cause problems. Any help they can get from any spirit is a good thing.

The challenge is, new Thai believers still possess the residue of their old, pre-Christian beliefs about the spirit world. They remain receptive to help from all sorts of spiritual sources. In their former lives, they commonly would have hung charms on their wrists, necks, the walls in their houses, or the rearview mirrors in their cars to obtain protection and blessing, and at times we have found that ongoing involvement in these old beliefs results in demonic influence in people's lives. (See Chapter Six.)

One of the most common ways to purportedly receive blessing, protection, and good fortune is through a *sai sin* bracelet. Monks bless white braided string bracelets and then tie them to people's wrists as they pronounce blessings and protection against evil. It is a common practice that many Thais understand as a custom rather than something spiritual. Sometimes new Christians go to temples to receive *sai sin* bracelets when they need boosts of good fortune. Well, you might ask, what's wrong with being blessed?

Jesus' teaching about the Greatest Commandment (Matthew 22:37) was based on the first of the Ten Commandments, which says, "You shall have no other gods before me" (Exodus 20:3). The Old and New Testaments affirm this commandment over and over. Yahweh God is the one and only God for His people. Jesus confirmed that He was the only path to God (John 14:6). When facing down the enemy, Jesus rebuffed Satan's offer to worship him by saying, "It is written, 'You shall worship the Lord your God, and him only shall you serve'" (Luke 4:8). Worshiping, serving, trusting in, or following any other spirit being is completely and categorically intolerable by scriptural teaching.

The act of requesting a favor from any being other than God implies trust in or reliance on that being. It places the favor-giver in the role of benefactor and the favor-receiver in the role of supplicant. Whether or not a *sai sin* bracelet was blessed by a monk in a temple, receiving it expresses trust in something besides God. I can't help but notice that knocking on wood, carrying rabbits' feet, crossing one's fingers, consulting horoscopes and fortune cookies, and observing other good luck superstitions seem quite similar to the *sai sin* ceremony. Where are we placing our trust—in God or in charms?

I'll take this line of reasoning one step further. Suppose you received a *sai sin* bracelet one day. You didn't really believe in its ability to help you, but you thought it couldn't hurt anything to accept it. Later that day something incredibly wonderful happened to you. Would you suspect just a little bit that the bracelet had a part in the blessing? If so, you would probably feel somewhat grateful to the bracelet. Gratitude translates into a sense of obligation, and obligation places us *under*, not *over*, the benefactor, which in this case is the bracelet. But God and God alone is the source of every blessing in our lives. Do not place your trust in any other god or benefactor.

DON'T WORSHIP ANGELS

According to Scripture, we are to worship God alone, placing ourselves under His power. Nothing else in all of creation is to be worshiped. Even the highest angels in their power and glory are off-limits when it comes to worship. In the process of writing the Book of Revelation, the apostle John found himself face-to-face with a powerful angel and in awe fell down at his feet in worship. Immediately the angel responded, "You must not do that! I am a fellow servant with you and your brothers who hold to the testimony of Jesus. Worship God" (Revelation 19:10).

There is a sense of urgency in the angel's response to John's worship. "Stop it! Stand up!" The angel's words indicate a hierarchical order in which angels and humans exist as fellow servants under the lordship and leadership of God. Angels are not to be worshiped, and in fact, Scripture never instructs humans to pray to or even put their trust in angels.

I have come to believe that God's hierarchy places humans positionally higher than all other created things—including angels. Hebrews 2:7 raises questions about that stance by describing Jesus in human form as "lower than the angels," but the writer was quoting Psalm 8:5, written by David to praise God for humankind's exalted position over all created things. The Hebrew word David used, *Elohim*, is translated "heavenly beings" and is not the word typically used for "angels." *Elohim* is often used as a reference to God, and several biblical versions translate it as "God" in this verse. (See NASB, NLT, CSB, and others.) David focused on the fact that God made human beings lower than *Himself* to steward His creation, but the writer of Hebrews highlighted something besides hierarchical order, namely that Jesus came to earth as a human being rather than an angel or heavenly being.

Like humans, angels are created beings. They have various roles throughout the Scriptures, including executors of God's judgment (the Passover angel in Exodus 12:23), messengers (Jesus' birth announcement angels in Luke 2:8-15), protectors (guardian angels in Psalm 91:11), and worshipers (Revelation 5:11-12).

Angels are *above* humans in physical and spiritual abilities, but Scripture makes it clear that angels do not share the incredible status held by redeemed humankind. Hebrews 1:13-14 states that angels are not heirs of God but are "ministering spirits sent out to serve for the sake of those who are to inherit salvation." Praise God that as believers we hold the elite designation of "children of God" (John 1:12) and "heirs of God and fellow heirs with Christ" (Romans 8:17) who will "inherit the kingdom prepared for [us] from the foundation of the world" (Matthew 25:34). Angels do not hold the rank of sons and daughters of God.

It's amazing to think that you and I are God's ultimate creation! We are His supreme handiwork. Nothing God created is higher than we are. As children of God, worshiping other created things—such as idols, people, ideals, habits, or anything else—is not only an act of disobedience to God's direct command, but it upsets God's created order. (See Romans 1:18-25.) Worshiping created things means placing oneself and one's trust under something intrinsically lower than oneself. Scripture clearly forbids it. We must worship God alone!

GOD INHABITS WORSHIP

Worship is extremely important to God. He loves worship so much that He instructed Moses to construct candlesticks to burn continuously in the Old Testament Temple with no end date. Heaven has the same worship orientation. Revelation 4:8 reveals that worship surrounds God's throne day and night without ceasing. Jesus confirmed God's desire for worship by stating that the Father is seeking true worshipers (John 4:23).

Scripture shows us how worship moves God to action. As worshipers lifted their praises to God and marched in front of Jehoshaphat's army, God caused the enemy soldiers to annihilate one another and gave victory to Israel (2 Chronicles 20:21-23). As David played his lyre, a harmful spirit left King Saul (1 Samuel 16:23). As Paul and Silas sang praises to God in the Philippian prison, God caused an earthquake to free them from their fetters (Acts 16:25-26). God responds to worship.

The Bible says when we worship God, His presence draws near to us. Psalm 100 says worship is the correct way to enter God's presence: "Come into his presence with singing!… Enter his gates with thanksgiving, and his courts with praise" (verses 2,4). The psalmist was describing people coming through the gates of the Jerusalem Temple and moving closer and closer to the Holy of Holies where the presence of God was located.

An attitude of praise and worship was—and still is—the appropriate way to approach God. Now the presence of God is located within us, and worship is still the key to access His presence and experience intimacy with Him.

Psalm 22:3 presents another metaphor about the role of worship: "You are holy, enthroned on the praises of Israel." As we worship we build a throne for God's presence to be seated above us. He responds and draws near as we worship Him.

So what does this have to do with idols and demons? Worship comes from our spirit, and He responds with His presence. On the other hand, when we worship idols or anything besides God, the demonic realm responds, just as it did in Corinth in Paul's time. As millions of Thai people bow to idols day after day, their veneration effectively invites the presence of demons to possess the idols and objects they worship.

We must be careful of the people or objects toward which we direct our worship. Our human spirits are powerful. When we worship God alone, His presence becomes available to us. Extended times of intentional worship bring us close to God, no matter how far from Him we may feel. If your prayers seem like they are going nowhere, worship God, and He will respond to you with the nearness of His presence.

WORSHIP IS AN ACT OF THE WILL

The first Chi Alpha[8] small group I attended at the University of Minnesota challenged my personal worship culture. Six or seven guys sat cross-legged on the floor of one of the student leader's apartment, and we studied Psalm 63:4: "I will bless you as long as I live; in your name I will lift up my hands." The leader reviewed various verses instructing us to lift our hands in worship and then asked us to practice lifting our hands to God in worship—

_____

8 Chi Alpha is an Assemblies of God ministry to university students.

something that made me more than a little uncomfortable. For 60 seconds we were to lift both hands high while we sat in place with our eyes open and our mouth closed.

I grew up in a reserved Scandinavian-background family. We religiously attended a conservative Pentecostal church in Little Falls, Minnesota. To put it mildly, we were not demonstrative in worship. When I was in my early teens, one of the older kids, Arlen Norwood, returned home from Evangel College (now University) in Missouri for summer break. At church on Sunday morning, Arlen sat near the front and raised his hands during worship. Everyone noticed. Many felt uncomfortable. I thought to myself, "What a show-off! He just wants us to notice how spiritual he is now." I think I believed raising one's hand was comparable to a spiritual gift. If God wanted me to raise my hand, it would float up on its own. I refused to fake it.

I don't know how the other guys felt in my Chi Alpha small group that evening, but I didn't want to do it. As I lifted my hands, they felt heavy. I felt insincere and wondered if I was guilty of sacrilege. Sixty seconds is a long time. But as we sat in a circle holding our hands in the air, a realization came over me. Maybe it was the voice of the Holy Spirit. I realized this group of guys with their hands in the air was a pleasing sight to God. I was almost overwhelmed with a sense of God's pleasure in us.

I learned that evening that worship is an act of the will, and our bodies are instruments of worship. There are dozens of Psalms that instruct us to worship God with our bodies. Besides raising our hands, we are told to clap, dance, sing, shout, prostrate, bow, kneel, and play instruments to God. None of the instructions mention waiting for inspiration before performing these acts of worship. Whether we feel a worship anointing fall upon us or not, we can choose to express worship to God. Consider the Levite families who were assigned as singers in the Temple in Jerusalem. Their job was singing day and night (1 Chronicles 9:33). Whether they felt like it or not, they sang worship to God, and He was honored.

We can and should worship God with our bodies. Paul writes, "You are not your own, for you were bought with a price" (1 Corinthians 6:19-20). Jesus purchased us—our whole selves, including bodies, souls, and spirits. We don't own our bodies. They belong to Jesus. Therefore, Paul goes on to say, "glorify God in your body."

One of Bangkok's most popular places of idol worship is Erawan Shrine, located on a busy intersection near the heart of the city. Its supposed ability to answer worshipers' prayers is known throughout the nation, resulting in a steady stream of visitors. The smell of incense permeates the air from early morning to late at night. A live band plays traditional Thai instruments while a line of costumed dancers weaves in worship to Lord Brahma the Great. People pay the dancers to thank the idol for answering their prayers, kneel with burning incense clasped between uplifted hands, or touch their foreheads to the ground.

People use their bodies to demonstrate obeisance to the idol—unmistakable acts of worship. Misplaced worship has a powerful effect, and the presence of darkness is strong there. Deliberately and humbly placing one's body in a worshipful attitude is powerful, and as Christians, we should do this before the Almighty Creator of the universe!

Today I make it a practice to kneel, bow, and lift my hands in worship, whether in public or in private. I have found that doing these things in my private prayer closet is usually more meaningful than during public worship. My body belongs to Him, and I willingly posture it in worship to Him. At times I don't say anything but simply lift my hands to Him in worship. When I do those things, I usually sense God's pleasure towards me and am drawn into His presence.

Worship is powerful. When people worship inanimate objects, demonic spirits respond. But praise God, when we worship Him, He responds! Worship God. Our deliberate worship moves Him.

SPIRITUAL INSIGHTS & PRAYERS

God created humankind as His highest creation and as spiritual beings who possess the ability to communicate with the unseen spiritual realm. Worship is the primary language in that realm, whether we are communicating with the Creator or with the things He created. As Buddhists worship created things, their enslavement to demonic powers deepens. As believers worship God, their relationship with Him grows stronger.

PRAY FOR BUDDHISTS

As Buddhists bow before idols, open their minds to the revelation they are slipping deeper and deeper underneath the influence of dark powers that control them rather than giving them freedom. May they recognize that idol worship is enslaving them spiritually and have courage to stop honoring idols and begin to pursue You.

PRAY FOR MISSIONARIES

I pray missionaries and Christian workers who live among idol worshippers will worship You with increasing intensity and that Your presence within and around them will increase so that everyone around them will sense the powerful presence of the Holy Spirit.

PRAY FOR YOURSELF

I pray my worship of You will grow in consistency. As I worship, fill me and my family with Your presence in increasing measure. May the presence of the Holy Spirit inside me become more and more obvious to people around me.

CHAPTER FOUR
THE GOSPEL DOESN'T MAKE SENSE

"If I invite my neighbors to my home, would you be willing to come tell them how to become Christians?"

I could hardly believe my ears! I had never received an invitation to share the gospel quite like that—and I haven't received another one since. It came from Pat, a Thai woman who served as a janitor at TLC Church. She was from a small village in the foothills just outside of Chiang Mai.

We had been living in Thailand for just over 10 years. Our first church plant, TLC Church, was doing great, pastored by a wonderful young couple who we had the privilege of mentoring (and matchmaking), King and Apple. We hired Pat two years earlier as our part-time housekeeper and church janitor. We grew close to her over the years and had many opportunities to share the gospel with her.

One day Pat surprised us by saying she loved Christians and wished she could be one. Wow! "You can!" I responded enthusiastically. It seemed too good to be true! Here was a Buddhist woman wanting to become a Christian in one of the most challenging places for the gospel.

"No," she laughed. "It is impossible for me to be a Christian."

"Yes, you can be a Christian," I insisted. "Becoming a Christian is something that happens in your heart. You can choose to give your life to Jesus and follow His ways. He forgives your sins. He lives in you. That is what it means to be a Christian."

Pat told me I didn't understand the challenges of becoming a Christian in her village and that it was out of the question.

Every now and then, Pat mentioned her desire to be a Christian, but no matter how hard I tried to convince her otherwise, she held strongly to her belief that it was not possible because of the pressures of the village and its leadership. I wasn't getting the whole picture, but we prayed for Pat's salvation regularly.

One day in 2006, Pat came to me with her big proposal. She wanted to get several of her close neighbors to come to her house so Janie and I could meet with them and teach them how to become Christians. Then perhaps they could all agree to become Christians together as a group. That, she believed, would make it possible for them to live as Christians in her village.

"Would you be willing to do that?" she asked me.

I responded, "Mmmm...let me think." No, I didn't! I said, "Yes, absolutely!"

We made plans to meet every Thursday evening at Pat's house in Ban Pong village to discuss what it means to be a Christian. As Janie and I drove the curvy roads up the mountain to Ban Pong the first Thursday evening, we wondered if any of Pat's neighbors would be there. If so, would they be receptive to us? This was a first for us, and we were nervous.

We pulled up to the tiny house and noticed several people hanging around. They smiled at us—a good sign. There were about 15 people there that first evening, and for a little over two years we met each Thursday night in Ban Pong to explain Christianity to Pat and her neighbors.

The Ban Pong experience taught us countless cultural lessons. We learned local temple abbots carry a huge amount of influence and could effectively provide constant opposition against us and our efforts. We learned about public shaming in an "honor-shame" culture like Thailand's when Pat and her neighbors were regularly singled out over the village public address broadcasts as embarrassments to the village. We learned there are many ways to cause problems—including legal problems—for Christians, even though it is not illegal to propagate the gospel in Thailand. Most of all, we learned the gospel as we presented it in America does not make sense to Thai people. During our two-plus years there, it seemed like every biblical concept we presented was misunderstood on some level and had to be dissected and rephrased, sometimes multiple times, until the people understood.

HOW *NOT* TO SHARE THE GOSPEL

Preparing for that first Thursday evening in Ban Pong, I knew if Pat and her neighbors were to fully understand the gospel, they had a lot of learning to do. They did not grow up with the cultural beliefs about God that most Americans understand, including God's existence as a personal being, His nature (Creator, Savior, omnipotent, etc.), heaven and hell, one life to live, and a plethora of other things. I knew I had my work cut out for me as I considered the expansive gaps between their worldview and mine. I wondered where to begin.

I knew I could not start with the most memorized verse in the Bible. John 3:16 wouldn't make sense to Pat and her friends, because without a Judeo-Christian foundation, their Buddhist worldview would likely result in a misinterpretation of nearly every phrase. Allow me to explain how John 3:16 might be misunderstood by Buddhist ears.

> *For God so loved the world, that he gave his only Son, that whoever believes in him should not perish but have eternal life.*

"FOR GOD"

The first two words of John 3:16 are confusing to Buddhists. The word *God* in Thai is *prajow*. It is used to describe powerful spirit beings, and as in all forms of Asian Buddhism, that means a lot of gods. Buddhism's founder, Siddhartha Gautama, was born and raised a Hindu, and many Hindu concepts carried over into Buddhism, including the concept of a heavenly level of existence where the gods live. Among the myriads of gods in the Buddhist world, none are like the Almighty God who created the world, exists eternally, and is entirely holy. None.

Thai Buddhists define the gods as powerful spirits that may have the ability to intervene in the human realm. They can be helpful to people who are nice to them and harmful to others. They are generally fearsome and unapproachable. People appeal to the gods when they are in trouble or when they need help beyond natural means.

Buddha did not claim to be a god but an ordinary human being who supposedly discovered truth without help or inspiration from the spiritual realm. He was simply a human trying to show other humans how to attain enlightenment. He taught that enlightenment happens entirely through human effort and focus. In fact, Buddha believed it is not possible for gods to attain enlightenment—only humans can. Gods must be reborn as humans to have the potential for enlightenment.

Not only did Buddha deny that he was a god, but his teachings suggested that if God exists, He is evil! When Buddha supposedly attained enlightenment under a fig tree, he began teaching The Four Noble Truths, which today provide the foundation of Buddhist teaching.

THE FOUR NOBLE TRUTHS

1. Life is suffering.
2. Suffering is caused by desires.
3. Suffering is extinguished by extinguishing desires.
4. Desires are extinguished by following the noble eightfold path.

The first of those truths is, *Life is suffering*. Buddha explained that life starts in a painful birth canal process, is replete with suffering experiences, ends in pain and death, and repeats the same torturous process in a perpetual cycle of suffering called *samsara*. The ultimate goal of Buddhism is to escape this miserable cycle of existence. Supposedly, a disciple once asked Buddha if God existed. Buddha responded that if a spirit powerful enough to create the world existed, he was an evil spirit, because he created a world of pain and suffering.

How would you like to live with that worldview? Life is suffering, I'm trapped in it, and my chief goal is to escape into nonexistence. This is one of the starkest contrasts between Christian and Buddhist worldviews. Christianity calls us to embrace our lives, our emotions, the world around us, and the God who made it all, while Buddhism calls us to reject it all as suffering, illusionary, and full of ignorance.

God created this world for us to enjoy, rule, and ultimately inherit. Jesus said, "I came that they may have life and have it abundantly" (John 10:10). I know He was talking about spiritual life, but unless you're a gnostic who separates your spirit from your body and soul, this means *all* life, including the spiritual and physical realms. God wants you to celebrate life "to the full, till it overflows" (AMP). Embrace it! Love it! Thank God for the world He made for us!

Before we share the gospel with Buddhists, we must understand their perspective of God. Buddhists will most likely not be interested in meeting the creator of the cycle of birth, death, and rebirth. To them, this creator is a sadist, inventing a perpetual trap and placing us in it.

Perhaps there are other people around us who view God in similar ways. Pursuing a relationship with God is not appealing to them because they misunderstand His attitude towards us and the world He created. Be sensitive to that possibility. Don't force God on them without trying to help them see that God is not the author of pain and suffering. God intends nothing but the best for His children!

Janie and I knew we could not start teaching Pat and her neighbors about Jesus without first building an understanding of who God is and why He created us.

"SO LOVED THE WORLD"

Believe it or not, love is ultimately a *bad* thing in Buddhism. The second, third, and fourth Noble Truths in Buddha's basic teaching identify *desire* (or craving) as the ultimate cause of suffering. As such, desire must be eliminated from one's life to stop the suffering. Buddha believed desires trap a person inside the perpetual cycle of birth, death, and rebirth. They are like glue, attaching a person to life, and only by extinguishing these desires can one hope to escape. One's emotions, wants, pursuits, and needs must be extinguished if one hopes to escape suffering. He claimed that when a person has successfully removed all his or her desires, no longer wanting, seeking, needing, or grasping anything, only then is that person able to escape existence and suffering.

Most would consider love to be a positive desire, but it is indeed a desire. As such, Buddhism considers it a craving that attaches a person to this suffering existence.

Years ago the Thailand Department of Religion in Bangkok conducted an interfaith discussion between Buddhist, Hindu, Muslim, and Christian leaders. One of the first questions was, "What is the highest concept of your religion?" The Christian representative explained that love was the highest concept of Christianity. God loves the world so much that He gave His only Son to die in our place, and God's great love lives in Christians, who are called to love all of humanity as much as we love ourselves

The Buddhist monk answered next. He explained that love is a weakness and demonstrates a person has not yet conquered that part of his or her emotional being. Love is an extremely challenging craving to conquer, he said, but when one reaches the higher levels of mindfulness, one can overcome the need to love and be loved. At that stage, one is nearing ultimate enlightenment.[9]

When Christians declare that God passionately and sacrificially loves the world, Buddhists may see His love as a weakness not a strength. Their example, Buddha, is above emotion. He is focused, unflinching, unmoved by pain and suffering, and completely absent of the need to be loved. This is the state of mind that all Buddhists seek to attain. Since the Christian God is not at all like that, they can only conclude that God has a long way to go to attain enlightenment.

Despite the Buddhist value of detaching from all desires, I have observed that the most powerful witness in Thailand is a loving Christian community. Thai people want to be loved just like people all over the world. God is love, and He created humankind to be just like Him. Christians know how to love others deeply and sincerely, and that is attractive to Buddhists.

---

9 Wan Petchsongkram. *Talk in the Shade of the Bo Tree.* Translated and edited by Frances E. Hudgins. (Bangkok: Thai Gospel Press, 1975), p. 47-48.

During a Friday evening prayer meeting at TLC Church in Chiang Mai, I asked the group of 15 or so Christians gathered there, "What brought you to faith in Jesus?" Two or three said it was when Jesus answered their prayers for miracles. The rest of them said the primary reason was the love and kindness of Christians towards them. Buddhists desire love, but in sharing the gospel with them, we must be sensitive to the values they have been taught.

God is love. He made us to love others and desire to be loved. Embrace it!

Despite the Buddhist value of detaching from all desires, the most powerful witness in Thailand is a loving Christian community. Thai people want to be loved just like people all over the world. God is love, and He created humankind to be just like Him.

"THAT HE GAVE HIS ONLY SON"

To effectively build a new understanding of God and the universe He created, Janie and I could not start our gospel presentation with the claim that God exists and that He loves people. But what could be wrong with telling Buddhists about the cross of Calvary and the incredible sacrifice Jesus made on behalf of humankind? Christ's atoning work is the greatest story ever told when seen through the lens of our Christian worldview.

Guess what? The crucifixion scene can be a stumbling block to Buddhists if not explained carefully.

The law of *karma* is a prominent concept in all strands of Buddhism. As a spiritual principle of cause and effect, it purports that a person's current existence—the quality of life in the *samsara* cycle of birth, death, and rebirth— reflects the cumulative deeds and intents of his or her past lives. If this life is filled with good things, like wealth, health, and power, it is merely reflecting good *karma* from the sum of good deeds from previous lives. On the other hand, if this life is filled with poverty, sickness, and pain, one has bad *karma* and is paying for bad previous lives.

Here's a sad statistic: Thailand leads the world in motorcycle accident deaths. Seventy percent of the nation's traffic deaths result from motorcycle accidents, numbering about 15,700 in 2018.[10]

Gruesome accident scenes were not uncommon to Janie and me as we drove Thai roads. Over the years we learned *karma* impacted the way Buddhists perceived these scenes. As we drove around bodies lying on the road in pools of blood, our hearts wept knowing 99.3 percent of Thai people did not have a saving knowledge of Jesus. The possibility that person was starting the rest of eternity in heaven was miniscule. We cried for the families who would miss them and for all the pain surrounding this tragedy.

However, people viewing the same accident scenes through *karma* lenses saw it differently. *Karma* told them the accident victims were reaping the effects of accumulated bad deeds and intents from previous lives, meaning they deserved it. They must have done many horrible things in their previous lives to deserve such painful deaths. In fact, *karma* told them the violence of the death indicated the victims were violent people in their previous lives. This view of death contributes to the fact

10 https://www.thaiwebsites.com/caraccidents.asp. Accessed 7/13/20

that newspapers in Thailand are not shy about publishing photos of grisly accidents.

The cross of Calvary represents a scene of intense, violent suffering. Mel Gibson's *The Passion of the Christ* was quite popular in Thailand, depicting blood and gore in far more detail than I wanted to see. Jesus suffered agonizingly. Grossly. Horribly. To me the crucifixion is more precious than anything else in the world. I cried when I watched the movie, and my eyes are tearing up as I write these words. Charles Wesley said it well: "Amazing love! how can it be that Thou, my God, should die for me?"[11]

But that is not how Buddhists are likely to interpret the scene at Golgotha. They see Jesus' brutal suffering and death on the cross as fitting payment for horrible *karma*. They suspect He was reaping the results of an incredibly evil prior life, including the likelihood that He was a mass murderer or something worse. The awesome love, grace, and mercy demonstrated in the passion of Christ may be completely lost if we describe the precious redemption scene without understanding the Buddhist perspective.

"SHOULD NOT PERISH BUT HAVE ETERNAL LIFE"

"How many rebirths must I expect to endure before I attain enlightenment?"

The Buddhist monk who was asked this question responded that the number of lifetimes one has to live to attain enlightenment compares to the number of times an eagle has to brush the peak of Mount Everest with its wing to flatten it to sea level.

Various branches of Buddhism define *enlightenment* in their own unique ways, but in general it is considered the eternal reward. Becoming enlightened results in *nirvana*, or the cessation of rebirth and suffering. According to Buddhist teaching, it took Buddha hundreds of lifetimes to attain enlightenment. Thai Buddhists following the

11 Charles Wesley. "And Can It Be, That I Should Gain?" (1738).

Theravada school of Buddhism believe only the highest monks have a chance at enlightenment in their present lifetimes. Everyone else must endure countless rebirths and practice right living and merit-making in this world of suffering to have any chance of enlightenment.

The promise that believers in Jesus "should not perish but have eternal life" understandably may not be viewed by Buddhists in a positive light. In their belief system, they already have eternal life. It is their goal to *escape* the endless cycles of birth, death, and rebirth. Eternal life is not a motivation to become a Christian; it is a stumbling block of misunderstanding that must be overcome.

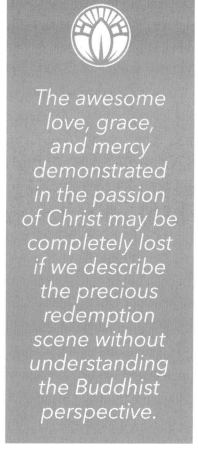

The awesome love, grace, and mercy demonstrated in the passion of Christ may be completely lost if we describe the precious redemption scene without understanding the Buddhist perspective.

Nirvana and heaven accentuate the contrast between Buddhist and Christian worldviews. One represents an escape from life, and the other embraces life eternally. Buddhism sees life as ignorant, illusionary, and full of suffering. Christianity sees life as created by God, valuable, and precious. Buddhism attempts to detach from life, extinguishing desires and the awareness of existence. Christianity attempts to embrace life, to fill the earth and take care of it, to love people, and to love the Creator. Ultimately, Buddhism seeks enlightenment that ends rebirth and existence. The goal is nothingness. Christianity seeks life everlasting with God in a place of unimaginable beauty without death, mourning, crying, or pain (Revelation 21).

At its core, Buddhism does not embrace God or the universe He created but instead denies their existence. While Buddhism and Christianity share many values, including moral standards and loving relationships, the core beliefs of the two systems could hardly be more divergent. There is no such thing as a Buddhist Christian.

WHERE WOULD WE START?

Back to the original question. As Janie and I sat down in Pat's living room that Thursday evening to explain Christianity, where would we start? Not with John 3:16.

SPIRITUAL INSIGHTS & PRAYERS

Because of their worldview, Buddhists may misunderstand the precious gospel message. They may view God as evil, love as weak, the cross as bad karma, and eternal life as a trap. Communicating the gospel to Buddhists in an understandable way requires cultural insight and, more importantly, divine inspiration. God's plan of salvation surpasses cultural barriers, and those who effectively communicate the message need Holy Spirit guidance.

PRAY FOR BUDDHISTS

I pray for Buddhists who misunderstand the gospel because of their worldview. Holy Spirit, please reveal God's amazing love for them and the wonder of Jesus' atoning work on the cross. May the gospel message make sense to them, and may they place their faith in You.

PRAY FOR MISSIONARIES

I pray missionaries and Christian workers will communicate the gospel message to Buddhists in a culturally contextualized and divinely inspired way, so they will understand its true meaning. Fill believers with wisdom and anointing as they witness. I pray Colossians 4:3-4 over them.

PRAY FOR YOURSELF

I pray for courage to build friendships with Buddhists. Give me opportunities to share Jesus with them, and teach me to be sensitive to their worldview and hear and follow the Holy Spirit's voice.

CHAPTER FIVE
GOD IS GOOD!

Historically, leading Buddhists to Christ in Thailand and most other Buddhist countries has been extremely difficult. The many conceptual misunderstandings we discussed in the previous chapter are partly to blame as well as powerful spiritual opposition from demonic activity like we discussed in Chapter Two.

Several other significant obstacles stand in the way of sharing the gospel with Thai Buddhists. First, Buddhism is part of Thailand's national identity. Thailand is Buddhist. On the country's tri-color flag, red stands for Thai people, blue for the king of Thailand, and white for Buddhism. For Thai people, rejecting Buddhism can feel equal to rejecting their homeland.

Second, Christianity is seen as a foreign religion, and many Thais believe it is not a valid option. They do not choose Buddhism; they are born into it. They are Buddhist by default, just as they believe Westerners are Christians by default.

There are many other obstacles, but the final one I'll mention here is the general belief among Thai Buddhists that their religion is older, more profound, and more broad-minded than what they consider to be the narrow, exclusive claims of Christianity. A former Buddhist monk, Wan Petchsongkram, stated, "Christianity is considered a religion of the ignorant and…is inferior to Buddhism both in moral requirements and in doctrinal profundity."[12]

In the mid-1830s Thailand's King Mongkut invited missionaries to work freely in Thailand without concern that they would convert Thai people to Christianity, saying, "What you teach people to do is admirable, but what you teach them to believe is foolish."[13]

Today, after nearly 200 years of missionary efforts, Thailand's population is less than one percent Christian.

With these giant obstacles looming over us and John 3:16 pulled out from under our feet, Janie and I began to share the meaning of Christianity with Pat and her neighbors in the village of Ban Pong.

We started with Genesis 1:1. "In the beginning, God created the heavens and the earth." We began building an understanding of our Creator as a wholly different spirit than the gods our Thai friends knew. In our first several meetings, we emphasized two characteristics of God that were especially significant for Thai Buddhists to understand. He is *eternal*, and He is *good*.

GOD IS ETERNAL

When you ask a Thai Buddhist how the earth came to be, they usually say, *gurt kheun ang*, meaning, "It happened by itself." Buddhists generally accept the big bang theory and Darwin's origin of life hypothesis. I personally suspect the principles of Buddhism discourage any sincere motivation to pursue other options, because they believe life is suffering, and nonexistence is better. Why should they make much effort to study where life came from?

---

12 Petchsongkram, p. 70.
13 Robert Bruce, "King Mongkut of Siam and His Treaty with Britain," *Journal of the Royal Asiatic Society Hong Kong Branch* 9 (1969): 91, https://hkjo.lib.hku.hk/archive/files/69fd1aab94ec2cfd112df0af2343fce4.pdf.

Former missionary to Thailand and my good friend, Ron Maddux, has an awesome sense of humor, and it extends to his preaching. When he preached to Thai Buddhists, he enjoyed bantering with them, and they would respond back to him.

He would ask, "How did the earth come to be?"

The crowd would respond, "It happened by itself."

"Where did the sun and moon come from?" Ron would ask.

"They happened by themselves."

"Where did people come from?"

"They happened by themselves."

Then Ron would take off his watch off and hold it high. "Where did this watch come from?"

"Japan? Switzerland?"

"It happened by itself," Ron would say.

The crowd would laugh and protest while Ron would ham it up by claiming that over millions of years of wind, rain, and earthquakes, the parts accidentally came together to form the watch.

Janie and I began by using Ron's illustration. The complexity of nature's design argues for a designer. The interdependence and balance of nature points to a purposeful planner. The beauty of the universe begs for a creator. Although the Ban Pong people had always been taught there is no creator, they agreed with what we said. It made sense to them that this world did not happen by accident. Indeed, it makes sense to anyone with an open mind.

"Our God," we told them, "is the Designer and Creator of the universe, but He is completely different from the gods you learned about in the temple. God is eternal."

The gods of Buddhism dwell in the heavenly realm, which is one of the six realms of existence within the *samsara* wheel of life. Buddhists believe the heavenly realm is a beautiful place where reborn people live as gods, reaping the rewards of previous good existences. These gods have limited lifespans, because those in the heavenly realm are still subject to the law of birth, death, and rebirth. They are destined to be reborn someday into another level of existence. Buddhism teaches that enlightenment can happen only at the human level, which means the gods must be reborn as humans to ever hope to attain enlightenment and escape *samsara*.

It is obvious to believers that the gods of Buddhism cannot compare with our almighty, eternal God. Before Buddhists can begin to understand the universe, the reason they exist, and God's purpose and plan for their lives, we must present God to them as completely apart from and above the gods they know.

> *Before Buddhists can begin to understand the universe, the reason they exist, and God's purpose and plan for their lives, we must present God to them as completely apart from and above the gods they know.*

It took two or three meetings to describe the eternal nature of our Creator God to the Ban Pong people. We told them He existed before humans and before the universe was formed. This was news to the villagers. They listened as though we were telling a magical fairy tale. Their imaginations were stretched to think about a God with no beginning and no end. It still stretches my imagination too!

A significant concept emerged as we talked about the eternal nature of God. He existed before sentient life (living, breathing beings), completely apart from Buddhism's *samsara* wheel of existence, which describes and explains the levels of sentient life. The idea was a revelation to them! Their interest was piqued to imagine a God who existed before life and before suffering, and they were paying close attention to our words.

GOD IS GOOD

Christians are taught that God is good. There is nothing *not* good about God. It may be difficult to accept this truth when we're experiencing periods of pain and suffering, but the principle of God's inherent goodness is an accepted belief.

Buddhists are taught that gods are like people; they possess both good and bad qualities and have good and bad days. Be careful not to stumble over a god on a bad day, or you will become an object of its wrath. This causes Buddhists to assume that if a creator god exists, he or she probably had a bad day when creating the world, because it is full of suffering and humanity is trapped here.

Good news! Our God is not like that!

When Janie and I introduced the concept that God is completely and entirely good, it was hard for our Ban Pong friends to swallow. It was an utterly different view of the gods. We explained that God created a good world, proving His own goodness, and we pointed to the perfect, unspoiled creation in Genesis 1-2 as evidence.

What was God's original intent for creation? Genesis 1 tells us God observed that what He made was *good*, implying satisfaction in His work. In fact, seven times in the creation account God called what He made *good*. His conclusion on the final day of creation was that it was *very good*.

"And God saw everything that he had made, and behold, it was very good" (Genesis 1:31).

Not only did God intend for creation to be good, but the Garden of Eden was a perfect paradise, a wonderful world entirely absent of suffering and death. Adam interacted with the animal kingdom, naming every living creature. Adam and Eve were completely innocent and unaware of even the possibility of sin and guilt. Animals didn't eat other animals (verse 30). There was no pain in childbirth. No laboring in the fields. No thorns or thistles. No relationship problems. No suffering.

When we look at Genesis 1–2, it is not difficult to perceive God's goodness. A good God created a perfect paradise—a preview of heaven. His goodness is a critically key concept for believers and is one of the foundational beliefs that separates Christianity from Buddhism. God's goodness makes it easy to embrace Him and His creation. It motivates us to get to know Him and pursue an intimate relationship with Him. It makes it easy for us to love Him and invite the world to love Him.

As Janie and I discussed God's goodness with our friends, we could see increasing interest in their eyes. They were considering the possibility of a Creator God who was not evil and did not create a system of pain and suffering.

WHERE DID SUFFERING COME FROM?

On week four or five, Janie and I finally made it to Genesis 3. This is one of the most pivotal chapters in the Bible for Buddhists, because it reveals the origin of suffering. Buddha defined *life* as ignorance and suffering. If suffering ceases, life ceases. Somehow in Buddha's search for truth he missed Genesis 1–2. Now Buddhists cannot imagine life without suffering.

We explained that world history changed the day Adam and Eve decided to disobey God and eat the forbidden fruit. Western Christianity defines this fateful day as the moment sin entered the world and tainted it forever. But in their Buddhist context, it was more understandable to say this was the day suffering began in the universe. Guilt possessed Adam and Eve when they recognized they had disobeyed their Maker, and in an attempt to hide their shame, they covered their naked bodies with leaves. From that day on, women were destined to bear children through pain and condemned to be controlled by men. The ground was cursed with thorns and thistles, and people were sentenced to expend great effort to grow their food. Old age and death entered the world for the first time (3:16-19).

As we described the origin of suffering, I could tell this was a brand-new concept for Pat and her friends. They had always been taught suffering defines life and cannot be separated from life. It just exists. They had never heard of the concept that suffering had a beginning. They were intrigued.

THE ANIMAL SACRIFICE PROBLEM

We moved on to Genesis 4 where Cain killed Abel out of jealousy when God favored Abel's offering over his. Cain offered a crop he had grown, while Abel offered the firstborn of his flock.

Surprisingly this story did not go over well with the Ban Pong people. They were shocked God would condone killing an animal. Just when they were beginning to accept God's existence and goodness, this account spoiled it all.

Buddhism's Five Precepts somewhat parallel the Ten Commandments. They are ethical guidelines all Buddhists are expected to follow. The first is, "Do not kill." Thai Buddhists say, *haam khaa sut*, which translates as, "Do not kill animals."

The first time I heard this, I asked my Buddhist friend, "What about people? Is there another command about not killing people?" My friend responded that animals and people are the same. They are both sentient beings living in the *samsara* wheel of life. In fact, it is possible for a person to be reborn as an animal in the next life if he or she is bad in the present life. Just like people, animals are working their way up the karmic ladder towards enlightenment. Killing them is just as much an act of murder as killing a human being.

BUDDHISM'S FIVE PRECEPTS

1. Do not kill.
2. Do not steal.
3. Do not commit adultery.
4. Do not lie.
5. Do not get drunk.

Does this mean Buddhists are vegetarians? No, not at all. Some sects refuse to eat meat, but most do partake. It is wrong to kill animals, but if someone else butchered the animal, it is not wrong to eat it. I have a hard time understanding how they can justify eating something that has been killed in violation of their beliefs, but none of my Buddhist friends have a problem with it. At the same time, most of them would not kill an animal even for food. Some of my missionary friends have made the mistake of showing their deer kills to Buddhist friends. Believe me, that doesn't go over well. Even fishing is viewed as murder.

One day I was eating lunch at an outdoor restaurant with some pastors, including Pastor Wirachai, the general superintendent of the Thailand Assemblies of God. We ordered fish, and as we sat chatting, we heard a loud pounding sound and turned to see the restaurant owner knocking a large fish over the head for our meal. "*Tham baab laew* (He just sinned)," Pastor Wirachai said jokingly. We all laughed, but his joke showed how deeply the concept of animal murder is fixed in Thai culture. Even though none of us believed the restaurant owner sinned by killing the fish, we all knew about and even felt the cultural guilt that comes with killing a living being.

During our early years in Chiang Mai, our good friends Sam and Shellie Bowdoin had a puppy that contracted a severe disease and was suffering horribly. They decided to put the puppy to sleep and drove to the local veterinarian. The vet refused to do it. Sam called several clinics but all refused. One told him to find a Christian or Muslim vet. Thai Buddhists fear taking the life of any living being will result in bad *karma*.

This explains why the Ban Pong people were confused when they learned that God refused Cain's grain sacrifice but accepted Abel's animal sacrifice. Why did God condone killing an animal? What's wrong with Him? How can He be good? We could tell they were seriously questioning whether the Christian God was a good one to follow.

This was another moment when Janie and I needed supernatural wisdom to respond to their questions. We needed prayer support! The Holy Spirit gave me an immediate answer, and again I knew someone was praying for us. Without hesitation I told them that for the next two weeks we would take some extended time to teach about two critical principles that would help them understand why God accepted Abel's sacrifice: the difference between animals and people and the fact that sin results in death.

ANIMALS AND PEOPLE ARE DIFFERENT

Growing up in rural Minnesota, my family always had one or two dogs. I still remember the Sunday afternoon our dog Penny died. She was a member of the family before I was born and lived to the age of 16. Mom and us five kids cried all afternoon. (Dad didn't ever cry, so that was no surprise.) We begged not to go to church that evening—even Mom didn't want to go—but Dad wouldn't hear of it, so we went, red-eyed and pitiful. We asked Mom if she thought we would see Penny in heaven someday. I can't remember exactly what she said, but it was something like, "No one knows for sure."

The Bible doesn't include a clear theology of animals, but the creation account clarifies that the man and woman were unique among all God created.

> *Then God said, "Let us make man in our image, after our likeness. And let them have dominion over the fish of the sea and over the birds of the heavens and over the livestock and over all the earth and over every creeping thing that creeps on the earth." So God created man in his own image, in the image of God he created him; male and female he created them. (Genesis 1:26-27)*

God created Adam and Eve to be unique in both function and essence. They functioned as leaders over the animal kingdom, but far more significantly, God created their essence in His own image. Of all God's creation, only humans reflect the image and likeness of God.

What exactly do *image* and *likeness* mean? Philosophers and theologians have debated this question for millennia. Some believe they imply humans can think and reason on a higher plane, while others believe they refer to the eternal souls of human beings or their ability to relate to God and each other in ways superior to animals.

Janie and I were not prepared to explore all the theological nuances of *image* and *likeness* with Pat and her friends, but we wanted to impress on them the fact that God made Adam and Eve like Himself in a way that was separate and different from the animals.

"What is the difference?" they asked. "Animals have arms, legs, eyes, ears, and hearts that pump blood throughout their bodies. They are sentient beings."

Another Holy Spirit moment happened. An illustration leapt to my mind. Someone was praying for us.

"Have you ever seen a monkey bowing down to an idol?" I asked them. There are still wild monkeys in Thailand, and several temples attract hundreds and even thousands of them. The Prang Sam Yod Temple in Lopburi has an annual monkey festival where tables of food are offered to hordes of monkeys, thanking them for the notoriety they bring to the temple. At Prang Sam Yod, monkeys unceremoniously climb all over the idols, but people are not allowed to disrespect the idols like that. In fact, tourists have been arrested and expelled from the country for climbing on idols.

"No!" Pat and her friends laughed out loud, imagining a monkey bowing before an idol.

"How about lighting incense or bringing an offering?" I asked. "Or just spending a moment in meditation? Have you ever seen a monkey do any of those things?"

"No! No! Monkeys don't do those things," they protested.

I tried to think of the next smartest animal. "How about dogs?" I asked. "There are lots of dogs at the temple. Have you ever seen a dog observing a religious ceremony?"

"Animals are not like that," they responded. Now they were teaching me. "They are not interested in religion."

Now came my punchline. "Then why do people everywhere in the world have gods and idols? Why do they pray and do other religious things? Why is it that when new people groups are discovered on tiny, remote islands of the Pacific, the people either have gods and idols to worship, or they worship the sun, stars, or other things in nature?"

They were stumped. "Why, teacher?"

"Because God created human beings with *spirits*."

I went on to teach that God created people in His image and likeness. He is spirit (John 4:24), and somehow He built a spirit-essence like Himself into our beings. The spirit part of us naturally desires spiritual interaction. It hungers for spiritual things and naturally seeks God. It is my theory that atheism does not come naturally. A person must be taught that the universe is merely physical, that all that exists can be explained scientifically, and that God is not necessary. Without this instruction, and often *despite* this instruction, people naturally assume a spiritual force much bigger than themselves exists and seek to interact with it, cry out to it in times of need, blame it for their pain, and hope it is real when they consider death.

Scripture teaches that we have an inner conviction that God is real. In fact, Paul implies that His existence is obvious:

> *For what can be known about God is plain to them, because God has shown it to them. For his invisible attributes, namely, his eternal power and divine nature, have been clearly perceived, ever since the creation of the world, in the things that have been made. So they are without excuse. For although they knew God, they did not honor him as God or give thanks to him, but they became futile in their thinking, and their foolish hearts were darkened. Claiming to be wise, they became fools. (Romans 1:19-22)*

Adam and Eve were different from the animals; they possessed spirits that related with God. They viewed the animal kingdom and the rest of creation as things to care for, and they viewed God as their Maker, Sustainer, and Lord.

Our Ban Pong friends seemed to understand the difference between animals and people. I asked them to keep that in mind as I taught them one other significant concept that would help them understand why God was pleased with Abel's animal sacrifice.

SIN RESULTS IN DEATH

During personal devotions one morning, a horrible feeling came over me. We had lived in Thailand at least

12 years at the time. I was reading about the dedication of Solomon's Temple in 1 Kings 8, and I almost shuddered when I read verse 63: "Solomon offered as peace offerings to the Lord 22,000 oxen and 120,000 sheep. So the king and all the people of Israel dedicated the house of the Lord." When I read that, I was taken aback at the massive loss of life, albeit animal life. This story had never affected me like that before, and I realized my reaction came from reading the story through the lens of a Thai person who believed killing animals was the same as killing people. Even though I knew the 142,000 animals sacrificed that day did not constitute mass genocide, I felt bad about it because of my cultural conditioning in Thailand.

How much more would my Ban Pong friends shudder at this story and others like it in the Old Testament? I knew I had to give them a clear explanation of God's rationale for animal sacrifice.

I asked them to turn to Genesis 2:16-17.

> *And the Lord God commanded the man, saying,*
> *"You may surely eat of every tree of the garden,*
> *but of the tree of the knowledge of good and*
> *evil you shall not eat, for in the day that you eat*
> *of it you shall surely die."*

The only prohibition in the Garden of Eden was the fruit of the tree of the knowledge of good and evil. Adam and Eve may not have understood what *evil* meant, but they understood clearly that they had two options: obey God and live or disobey God and die. The choice couldn't be clearer. What idiot would choose the latter? But when the serpent appealed to their curiosity and softened them up by questioning God's motive, they gave in and chose to disobey God's direct order.

For Pat and her friends, the key words in this Scripture were, "You shall surely die." Death accompanies disobedience. It's a scriptural principle. "The wages of sin is death" (Romans 6:23). Creator God promised Adam and Eve they would die if they ate the fruit of the forbidden tree. But the truth is, they didn't die right away! At least not physically. Scripture says until we are *born again* through the atonement of Jesus, our spirits are dead to God. Adam and Eve's spirits died when they bit into the fruit, but their bodies didn't die immediately. Why not?

Although Genesis 3 does not clearly spell out God's reason for allowing Adam and Eve to survive that day, Scripture eventually reveals His merciful strategy to spare their lives and billions of others to come. The apostle Paul tells us God had this loving, merciful, gracious plan in place before the world was formed (Ephesians 1:4). God became the man Jesus Christ and came to earth to die in Adam and Eve's place.

We told Pat and her friends about God's plan. We went back to the story of Cain and Abel in Genesis 4 and explained how God's plan depended on Cain and Abel's cooperation. For Cain and Abel to obtain forgiveness, they had to demonstrate repentance for their sins by providing a symbol of death. It would represent their death sentences and foreshadow the substitutionary death of Jesus in the distant future. The symbol must be something deeply meaningful and of great value. It made sense for God to choose the death of animals to represent humankind's death sentence and His eventual death on their behalf.

God did not take pleasure in the death of animals. His creation is precious, and Genesis 1 tells us He calls it *good*. In Psalm 19:1 creation "proclaims his handiwork." Isaiah 40:26 says God calls all the stars by name! Jesus taught that God feeds the birds, clothes the grass of the fields, and takes notice when a sparrow falls to the ground (Matthew 6:26–30; 10:29). God doesn't dislike or devalue animals. He said through the prophet Isaiah, "I do not delight in the blood of bulls, or of lambs, or of goats" (Isaiah 1:11). When He chose to represent His substitutionary death for humankind through animals, their deaths were truly meaningful sacrifices.

We told the Ban Pong group that God was sad animals had to die to represent Cain and Abel's sin, but this was part of His plan to pay for their sins and the sins of the whole world. They understood.

Something else occurred to me. "Who was the first one to take the life of an animal in the Bible?"

"Abel?" someone offered.

"Look at Genesis 3:21," I instructed them. "'The Lord God made for Adam and for his wife garments of skin and clothed them.' It is quite probable that God himself was the first one in the Bible to take an animal's life."

Some theologians caution us about reading too much into God's act of clothing Adam and Eve. Scripture doesn't specify the skins were from an animal, but the Hebrew word `ôwr, used here for "skin," is used exclusively in the Bible to refer to animal or human skin.[14] Certainly God could have created skins for clothing rather than taking them from a living being, but even though Scripture does not go into detail, it appears God took the life of an animal to cover Adam and Eve.

Adam and Eve had covered themselves with fig leaves after they sinned to hide the nakedness they had never noticed before. They must have felt desperately embarrassed, exposed, and guilty. They wanted to cover their sin. I don't blame them. They knew God had promised death for disobedience.

But instead of taking their lives, God cursed the tempter, promised a Savior, and covered their shame. Hallelujah! I cannot help but interpret the animal skin clothing as symbolic. He took the life of an animal to cover their guilt both physically and symbolically. Fig leaves were their feeble attempt to do what only God could do. Adam and Eve must have experienced a double shock that day. First

14 https://www.blueletterbible.org/lang/lexicon/lexicon.cfm?Strongs=
H5785&t=NIV, accessed 4/10/2021.

they realized they were not going to die. They had been spared certain execution. Then God created clothing for them out of animal skins. God's actions were full of meaning. The skins of that sacrificed animal represented the life-giving sacrifice of Jesus, the coming Savior who would cover shame and guilt once and for all.

From that day in the Garden of Eden until the day Jesus died on the cross, God accepted animal sacrifices to represent His substitutionary death. Every time an animal was offered to God as a sin offering, it reminded people of the high cost of sin and the mercy of Almighty God. But take notice! Despite the high cost, *none*— absolutely zero—of the millions of animals sacrificed in the Old Testament had the power to forgive people's sins. Hebrews 10:4 tells us, "It is impossible for the blood of bulls and goats to take away sins." Despite thousands of years of sacrifices and massive loss of animal life, forgiveness of sin could not and did not happen through the blood of bulls and goats.

Jesus provided the only substitutionary death that could forgive sins. God himself paid the penalty for the sins of all humankind throughout history. "By a single offering he has perfected for all time those who are being sanctified" (verse 14). Jesus' death covered Adam and Eve's guilt. Jesus' death covered Abel and those who followed him. The deaths of millions of animals before Jesus simply foreshadowed what was to come. *Jesus paid it all!*

GOD'S GOODNESS IN SPITE OF SUFFERING

When we finished explaining the difference between humans and animals and God's standard that sin demands death, our Ban Pong friends seemed to understand why God accepted animal sacrifices in the Old Testament. It was a lot to take in!

Looking back on our meetings in Ban Pong, I suspect there may have been a remnant of doubt in people's minds about God's goodness. It is one thing to conceptualize suffering entering the world because of sin but another to process the pure volume of pain and suffering in the world. Sometimes it can cause even the most ardent believer to question whether the Creator is altogether good.

In late December 2004, the infamous tsunami struck the southwestern coast of Thailand, killing over 5300 Thai people.[15] It devastated the ocean wildlife that provided livelihoods for most of the people along the coast. It ravaged people's land, homes, and boats and took the lives of friends and family.

Several of our missionary friends, including Dan and Gail Klepel, were among the many who helped in the relief efforts. Dan and Gail listened to story upon story of pain and tragedy and in great sympathy asked how they could help. They expected requests for food, water, shelter, and boats, but instead many people wanted answers.

Why had they suffered such a disaster? Was it bad *karma* catching up to them from previous lives? Were they being punished for some horrible sin?

Dan and Gail discovered some people had asked the same questions of Buddhist organizations offering help, but they were dissatisfied with the answer. The Buddhists had explained all this happened because of *karma*. The people who died violently and painfully had horrible *karma* from bad deeds in previous lives and deserved to die. But that explanation implied all the victims must have shared the same bad *karma*.

It didn't make sense, and they wanted to hear a Christian explanation.

What *is* the Christian explanation for the tsunamis in our lives? How can a good God allow tragedies like this to happen? Christians must reconcile God's goodness with the pain and suffering all around us.

15 "FACTBOX–Key Facts on the 2004 Tsunami," Reuters, March 11, 2011, https://www.reuters.com/article/idINIndia-55502220110311.

Dan and Gail told the people about God's good and perfect design for humankind. They described the serenity of the Garden of Eden and the paradise Adam and Eve enjoyed. There were no tsunamis, no death, no pain. They described Adam and Eve's rebellion against the Creator God and His judgment against them and the perfect world He had made. The resulting pain, suffering, and death continue to impact us all to this day. They explained it was not God's original plan for us to experience tsunamis, and someday God will restore the perfection of His original creation, and they could enjoy it if they entrusted their lives to Him.

Up and down the 100 miles of beach along the western border of Thailand, several churches were planted as people accepted the Christian explanation for the disaster they had endured. They could tolerate the pain when they understood why their friends and family had suffered and died.

As believers we understand, recognize, and agree that God is good—entirely good—and that His goodness includes justice and judgment of sin. Embracing God's justice as *good* is a subject well beyond the breadth of this chapter, but it's a concept Christians need to understand and accept. Thankfully, His justice leans sharply toward the side of mercy. God's just and merciful judgment spared Adam and Eve from immediate physical death, evicting them from the Garden of Eden instead. But their banishment introduced the horrible consequences of living in a world full of suffering.

We agree with Buddha that life is filled with suffering, but we disagree that suffering defines our existence. Suffering was not God's original intent for our lives. We know where it came from and why. We know it will end. And we know God has good plans for each of us. We know God is good!

SPIRITUAL INSIGHTS & PRAYERS

Buddhists teach that suffering and existence are inseparable. According to this reasoning, if a creator god exists, he is evil, because he created an existence of suffering. The concept of a good God is foreign to Thai Buddhists. To complicate this challenge, the Old Testament sacrificial system appears offensive to Buddhists who are taught that killing animals is murder, and it reinforces the notion that God is evil. However, Genesis 1-4 explains the origin of suffering and depicts God as completely good and abundantly merciful. Despite the reality of suffering in the world, God is good and desires good things for all people.

PRAY FOR BUDDHISTS

I pray for Buddhists who believe that if You exist, You must be evil, because You created a world of suffering. May they recognize Your goodness and turn to You for salvation.

PRAY FOR MISSIONARIES

I pray missionaries and Christian workers will operate in the gifts of words of wisdom and knowledge as they communicate the gospel to Buddhists. Inspire them with insightful, effective ways to teach about Your goodness despite the existence of suffering.

PRAY FOR YOURSELF

I pray when I am going through suffering and challenges, I will turn to You, sense Your comfort, and be reassured of Your goodness. When people around me suffer, show me how to encourage them and reassure them of Your goodness.

CHAPTER SIX
BELIEVERS OR SEEKERS?

Some Christians are super-evangelists. I'm talking about the kind of people who seem to be able to lead others in the sinner's prayer at the drop of a hat. I never possessed that gift.

During our furlough in 2002-2003, I served as the Missionary in Residence at Cedar Valley Church in Bloomington, Minnesota. Nearly every Monday during staff meeting, Tom, CVC's outreach pastor, had a new story of someone—and often several people—he had led in the sinner's prayer during the past week.

I admire Tom and super-evangelists like him, but I learned that in Thailand the sinner's prayer represents a tiny first step in a long discipleship process. Thai people would allow me to pray for them, but they didn't know to whom I was praying, why I was praying, what was expected of them, or what was supposed to happen to them when I finished praying. The process from Buddhist to true believer is long, slow, and arduous. Pastor Wirachai Kowae, the much-revered former Thailand Assemblies of God general superintendent, used to say the average time for a typical Thai Buddhist to become a mature Christian is seven years.

Up to this point in our Thursday evening Ban Pong studies, Janie and I had been thrilled with the progress we made. It took six or seven Thursday evenings to explain the creation account, the fall of Adam and Eve, the origin and cause of suffering, God's forgiveness demonstrated by animal sacrifice, the difference between humans and animals, and God's goodness. The Ban Pong people seemed to be following along and accepting everything we taught. Things were going well.

The next surprise happened one evening when we were still somewhere in Genesis 4. Pat interrupted my teaching by raising her hand.

"Teacher," she stated. "We are all ready to be Christians now. What should we do?"

Wow! My mind started to race. This was happening too quickly! We were still early in Genesis. I had not taught about Jesus yet. They hadn't heard about the baby in Bethlehem. They didn't know Jesus died on the cross in their place. They didn't know about His power to wash away sin. They had no clue what it meant to submit themselves to Jesus' lordship. How should I handle this? I couldn't tell them they weren't ready to be Christians.

I also suspected their motivations were not entirely pure. They were unhappy with the control of the local Buddhist abbot and his temple, especially the way they were forced to make contributions under the threat of public humiliation and evil spirit reprisals. They believed the Christian religion offered them freedom from the control and financial obligations of the Buddhist counterpart. What if this group decision to convert was more political than spiritual?

Once again I turned to the Holy Spirit for wisdom, and once again I am certain intercessors were calling out to God on our behalf. The answer came immediately and clearly. I told them they could indeed become Christians that very evening, but first they needed to understand two important things: Idols and God don't mix, and personal rights must submit to God's leadership.

IDOLS AND GOD DON'T MIX

Looking at the Ban Pong people around me, I suddenly became keenly aware of all the idols and charms in their lives. Thai people are surrounded by these objects. They grow up believing they contain genuine spiritual power to help them in their daily lives. Idols stand outside and inside their homes, workplaces, schools, government offices, and along the roads. They wear charms on necklaces and bracelets, have them tattooed on their bodies, and hang them in their vehicles. Idols and charms had always been normal for these people, and all of them owned some.

I announced that becoming Christians meant inviting the Creator God to be the *only* god in their lives. It meant shifting all their past dependencies on spirits, idols, and charms to trust in God and God alone. From now on, only God would provide for their spiritual and physical needs, including financial provision and protection over their homes, their cars, their families, their health, their businesses, and all their possessions. Idols and charms and their accompanying spirits are not compatible with God. It is impossible to simultaneously place trust in the Creator God and other spirits. Becoming Christians meant removing all idols, charms, and anything else they trusted in to provide for and protect them.

I asked if they were willing to make this commitment. The room was quiet. I had dropped one bombshell on them, and I had another yet to drop.

SUBMIT YOUR RIGHTS

Is salvation free? Preachers love to say God's grace means redemption is offered completely without charge.

I have preached that very thing many times. "**G**od's **R**iches **A**t **C**hrist's **E**xpense" is a catchy reminder that Jesus paid all the costs involved in saving us from the penalties of our sins. Romans 5:15-17 tells us righteousness is a "free gift," and Ephesians 2:8-9 reminds us we could never earn or deserve our salvation.

Yes, Jesus *did* take upon Himself our penalty of death, He *did* erase our sin and judgment, and He *did* offer righteousness to us free of charge. Yet as I sat in the circle of Ban Pong villagers that Thursday evening, I couldn't help but think of the commitment that would be required for them to receive that gift. They had to yield their rights to God, but standing in the way was something called *free will*.

Submission to Jesus' lordship is costly. It means we are conceding control, recognizing God's ownership, and giving up the "right" to be in charge. Jesus purchased us as His own property. "Do you not know that.... you are not your own, for you were bought with a price" (1 Corinthians 6:19-20). Salvation is free in terms of its transforming effect, but receiving it demands total surrender. It costs us something.

Perhaps we do them a disservice when we tell people becoming a Christian is entirely free of charge. In truth, they must be willing to give up ownership of their lives to God, submitting their free will and following His direction instead. That's expensive! Of course, placing their lives in God's loving, merciful, wise, and almighty hands brings the greatest of all rewards.

I explained to Pat and her friends that one decision remained. Becoming Christians that evening meant asking the Creator God to become the leader of all aspects of their lives—what to do, where to go, and what to say. Becoming Christians meant if God told them to sell their homes and move to another city, they would be willing to do it. It meant obeying all the Bible says as best they could.

"Are you ready and willing to remove all idols, charms, and anything else you trust for good luck or spiritual help and trust in God alone?" I asked.

It was quiet.

"And are you ready and willing to obey God in all things and follow the Bible's teaching as best you can for the rest of your lives? If so, then you are ready to be Christians."

It was still quiet.

I was hard on them, but I wanted them to know their decision meant far more than simply following a different religious path or making a political decision out of frustration. Choosing Christ would involve a sincere commitment to submit their wills to His lordship.

Submission to Jesus' lordship is costly. It means we are conceding control, recognizing God's ownership, and giving up the right to be in charge. Salvation is free in terms of its transforming effect, but receiving it demands total surrender.

I wasn't ready for Pat's counteroffer.

"Teacher, we would like to become Christians, but we aren't ready at this time to become radical Christians. Is there an entry level that would not require us to promise all those things to God now?"

BELIEVERS OR SEEKERS?

I almost laughed out loud at Pat's genuine and entirely innocent question. Was there a beginner-level commitment to Jesus that didn't demand everything? I was just about to tell her becoming a Christian meant total commitment when another idea leapt to mind. It was a radical idea. Was this the Holy Spirit speaking to me? Or was it just me? Was it heresy? I wasn't sure.

Someone was praying for us. Before I could think through all the questions, my mouth opened and I heard myself saying, "Yes, there is an entry level for you. If you are not ready to become a *believer* in God, you can be a *seeker* of God." I had never considered seeker-level Christianity, but without even thinking it through, I began to define what being a *seeker* meant.

I told Pat and her friends becoming seekers meant they were ready to promise me and God three things: 1) they would try their best to read their Bibles every day, 2) they would attend all our Thursday evening Bible studies as faithfully as possible, and 3) they would pray regularly, asking God to show them who He is, how to trust Him with their lives, and how to become true believers. If they promised to do these things, one day they would be ready to become true believers.

When I asked if they were ready to become seekers, they immediately agreed. Everyone was excited and confident they could commit to those three things. It was a group decision, which is normal in this part of Asia. Without being instructed, they all dropped to their knees, put their hands in a praying position, and looked at me for direction. I asked them to repeat this prayer after me:

> *Dear God, I promise from this day onward to do my best to read my Bible every day. I promise to attend Bible studies as faithfully as I can. I promise to pray regularly, asking You to*

*show me who You are and show me how to trust
You with my whole life, so that one day I will
become a true believer. Amen.*

Pat and her neighbors repeated each phrase
emphatically and sincerely. After their "amen," they all had
looks of accomplishment on their faces. They had entered
the Christian world in a culturally comfortable way, namely
through a religious ceremony.

It wasn't the *sinner's* prayer; it was the *seeker's* prayer.
We began to use it regularly with our Buddhist friends
who were drawn to Jesus but not ready to cut ties
with idols, spirits, or Buddhist practices. It may sound
questionable to some readers, but please indulge me for
a moment.

Becoming a Christian in America typically happens in
a moment of decision. A preacher, a friend, or the voice
of the Holy Spirit brings inner conviction, and someone
decides to confess sin and ask Jesus to be Lord and Savior.
That moment of decision is valid and relatively informed,
because most Americans have some idea who God is and
that He wants to interact with people. They have a concept
of His pure and holy nature compared to sinful human
nature. They realize their inherent right and ability to
change their allegiance from self or Satan to God.

But most Thai Buddhists understand absolutely none of
those concepts. If they were invited to pray the sinner's
prayer, many would do so gladly, because they believe
religious ceremonies benefit their lives, including their
health and finances. But after they prayed, most would go
merrily on their way to make merit at the temple, feeling
encouraged and hopeful the Christian god would give
them good luck. Many Thai Christians, committed to the
belief that salvation happens in a ceremonial moment,
bring their Buddhist friends and family members to
church and pressure them to respond to the altar call

for salvation. I have seen people pull their unwilling seatmates to the altar to repeat the sinner's prayer, convinced spiritual transformation would happen as the confession of faith was repeated.

Spiritual transformation can happen in the blink of an eye, but it often happens progressively as God draws people's hearts to Himself.

Of course, spiritual transformation can happen in the blink of an eye, but it often happens progressively as the Father draws people's hearts and minds to Himself (John 6:44) and faith is exercised (Ephesians 2:8). In the Thai Buddhist context, transformation is usually a longer process. I no longer wait until people are ready to become believers—understanding what Jesus did to pay for their sins and what commitment to His lordship means—before praying the sinner's prayer with them. Instead I ask as soon as possible if they are interested in becoming seekers, and I invite them to pray the seeker's prayer and commit to pursuing knowledge of God.

One Sunday morning three orange-robed Buddhist monks walked into TLC Church in Chiang Mai where we were ministering. They sat in the front row, which is expected of monks in Thailand. They are given special treatment everywhere they go and have front-row reserved seats on buses, trains, and planes. Subways and overhead rail systems have signs instructing people to vacate their seats for monks. They go to the front of all lines. So of course, they sat on the front row at church.

The members were excited but nervous. Should they *wai*[16] and bow to the monks as expected? Should they sing and worship God with their hands in the air as they would normally do? I understood their discomfort, knowing the cultural expectations, but I was thrilled the monks were there.

The pastor greeted the monks briefly and came to me with a nervous look on his face. "They asked if they could become Christians!" he whispered. "What should I tell them?"

Immediately a humorous picture came to mind: three monks renouncing Buddhism, removing their orange robes, throwing them in the garbage can next to the platform, and pledging to follow Christ the rest of their lives. It's humorous, first of all, because monks do not wear undergarments, so the robes were staying on. But on a deeper level, it wouldn't have happened anyway, because the monks did not intend to leave Buddhism or the monkhood to follow Christ. They had no clue what commitment to Christ meant. Their underlying question was whether monks were allowed to attend church and participate in Christian practices.

The answer is, "*Yes*, monks can become Christians!" Buddhist monks can become seekers and commit to attending church faithfully, reading their Bibles daily, and praying God would reveal Himself to them until they reach the point of becoming true believers—so can drug addicts, liars, adulterers, and all other sinners. No one has to clean up his or her life before becoming a seeker.

Unfortunately, the monks never came back to church. I don't know why. Maybe they weren't ready to be seekers yet. They certainly were not ready to be believers.

I have discovered the task of evangelism—especially in Thailand—is much easier when my goal is to identify *seekers* instead of *believers*. Myriads of people are curious

---

16 Bring one's hands up to the face in a praying position.

about Jesus, but most do not want to be pushed into a lifetime decision. That's understandable. They don't yet understand exactly what that would mean. But they might be ready to commit to seeking God, and the seeker status opens the door for discipleship, which I will discuss in the next chapter.

Eventually, Pat and some of her neighbors were ready to pray the sinner's prayer and become true believers. We discovered the transition from seeker to believer was unexpectedly challenging. Even though they faithfully followed through on their commitments as seekers, there were powerful barriers standing in the way. It took an incredible miracle for the first new believer to take the plunge.

SPIRITUAL INSIGHTS & PRAYERS

The Eastern Buddhist worldview is oceans apart from the biblical worldview. It can take many years for a Buddhist to understand what salvation and lordship mean. Rather than pressing them to pray the "sinner's prayer" when they don't fully comprehend the meaning of salvation, we invite them to pray the "seeker's prayer," pledging to search for God until they find Him. Then we faithfully disciple them until they voluntarily and knowingly place their faith in Jesus as true believers.

PRAY FOR BUDDHISTS

I pray thousands of Buddhists will grow curious about the Christian message. May they find a Bible or Christian literature that will attract their interest. Send believers to guide them to become seekers and help them pursue the knowledge of You.

PRAY FOR MISSIONARIES

I pray missionaries and Christian workers will have divine appointments with Buddhists who are ready to become seekers. Prepare them to lead these seekers to search until they find You as Savior and Lord.

PRAY FOR YOURSELF

I pray for the opportunity to meet Buddhist seekers who are curious about You. Help me be willing to spend time with them, show them who You are, lead them to trust in You, and guide them into growing as true followers.

CHAPTER SEVEN
BARRIERS

Sai worked as janitor at TLC Church before Pat came. Like Pat and 90-plus percent of Thai people, she was born and raised a Buddhist and considered Christianity a religion for foreigners—not her. Many Thais see Christianity not only as foreign but as a younger, inferior belief system. They point out that Jesus lived on earth long after Buddha (who died about 550 B.C.). They view Christians, Jews, and Muslims as weak, because they rely on a god to save them instead of doing it themselves. For these reasons and more, Sai was not at all receptive to the gospel when we first met her.

Janie and I slowly built a trusting relationship with Sai and learned more about her life. She had two daughters with different fathers, both of whom mistreated and left her. It took six or seven years before she was willing to discuss spiritual things with us, which is typical of Thai Buddhists. We were thrilled when she began attending church on Sundays, and even more so when she agreed to meet with us weekly for a simple evangelistic Bible study called *The Great Questions of Life*.[17]

We met with Sai for about an hour each week after work. We studied the nature of God, how the world began,

---

17 Global University. http://www.thegreatquestionsoflife.org/. Accessed 9/28/20.

where sin came from, and how God judged sin through Jesus' atoning work on the cross. After each lesson we asked Sai if she was ready to invite Jesus to live in her heart as her Savior and Lord. Each week she told us she was not ready.

One day the Holy Spirit directed our study in a supernatural way. Someone was praying!

We were studying the work of Satan in the world. I went down a rabbit trail, describing the difference between the Thai concepts of "ghosts" and "evil spirits." Most Thais are desperately afraid of ghosts, and some think they're hiding behind every tree and under every rock, yet they love to watch spooky movies. They believe ghosts are spirits of dead people hanging around to haunt them. If people have unfinished business before they die, they may tie up loose ends as ghosts. If they die with unsatisfied grudges, they may torment their adversaries with fear and disruption. If they die violently, they may create havoc as retribution. I explained to Sai that the Bible does not support the idea of ghosts, but it does teach that evil spirits live and work among us.

Many Thai people think foreigners (white foreigners anyway) do not believe in ghosts. After all, white foreigners will rent houses near cemeteries or where someone has been murdered, but Thais would never consider living there. In fact, rent at those places can be extraordinarily low, which is an advantage for those who are not afraid of ghosts.

Sai looked skeptical, so I repeated myself with emphasis. Ghosts are not real! The spirits that bother people are fallen angels who work under Satan's leadership to keep people from knowing and believing in God.

Sai surprised me with her next words. "I know ghosts are real," she said resolutely. When her beloved father passed away, her family gave her the responsibility to "take care" of him. She was to light incense and candles daily on the spirit shelf in her home where the urn holding her father's ashes stood. She also provided a fresh glass of water and a simple snack of some kind every day. The incense and candles displayed love and respect, and the water and snack provided for him in his afterlife realm. After taking care of these things each day, Sai would kneel, bow, and meditate briefly before her father's urn to honor him.

One day Sai was overcome with a painful headache. It was so bad she knew it wasn't a normal headache. It seemed evil. Maybe she had done something bad and was suffering the karmic consequences? Had she harmed someone? Had she mistreated her kids? Suddenly she realized she had forgotten to take care of her father that morning. A wave of fear came over her, and she dropped what she was doing and rushed home. She lit the incense and candles, placed the fresh water and food next to her father's urn, and knelt to meditate. Immediately the headache disappeared.

"So I know ghosts are real," she said confidently.

I asked the Holy Spirit to guide my next words. Yes, someone was praying for us.

"Did your father love you, Sai?" I asked her.

"Yes!" she answered emphatically.

"Was your father abusive? Did he beat you?"

"No!" Sai sounded a bit offended. For the sake of my next questions, I was really glad she didn't say yes!

"How do you think your father would respond if you forgot to bring him a glass of water and a snack? Do you think he would give you a painful headache?"

She hesitated. "Maybe not," she said quietly.

"That is not your father who gave you a headache, Sai," I told her. "I believe it is an evil spirit pretending to be your father. If an evil spirit can convince you it's your father, then it can manipulate you into serving and worshiping it every day." Sai was thinking quietly.

Then, I waded into deep water. I told her God is more powerful than any and all evil spirits, including the one pretending to be her father. I asked her to test God's power and stop taking care of her father for the next seven days. If she would do that, Janie and I would pray against the evil spirit—that it would have no more power to give her headaches or cause problems.

Sai didn't respond to my challenge. She was still thinking. But she didn't say no.

Janie and I prayed over her. We rebuked the evil spirit pretending to be her father and asked Jesus to surround her with His supernatural protection. We prayed she would not have headaches or any other problems in the upcoming week.

For the next seven days, Janie and I prayed fervently for Sai and asked our friends and supporters to pray with us. We were in a showdown with demonic powers.

I couldn't wait for our next Bible study with Sai. When we met, I blurted almost immediately, "Did you take care of your father last week?"

"No." She answered with a bit of a smile.

"Did you have any headaches?"

"No." Now she was really smiling.

"Are you ready to invite Jesus to live in your heart as Savior and Lord?" I knew the moment was right.

"Yes, I want to do that."

We led Sai in the sinner's prayer. She had believed in Jesus, perhaps for years, but her belief in ghosts was a barrier standing in the way of complete commitment to Him. When that barrier was removed, she was free to embrace saving faith in Jesus.

We discovered Sai's barrier battle is a common pattern among seekers. It seems that every person considering faith in Christ has something holding them back. It may be a conflicting belief, a nagging doubt, a confusing experience, a misunderstanding, or a relationship, but it is a barrier keeping them from submitting to Jesus. Since we became conscious of this pattern, we have gotten accustomed to praying for the Holy Spirit to reveal each barrier to us or the person making the decision. One of our supporters' primary roles is to pray the Holy Spirit exposes people's barriers, overcomes them, and opens their hearts to receive Jesus as Savior and Lord.

BODY DONATIONS

Barriers to salvation had been evident in Ban Pong for many months. Although Pat and all the other house church attendees had become enthusiastic *seekers* of God, they were not willing to take the next step as *believers*. I could not understand it. They wanted to be Christians. They identified themselves as Christians. They attended weekly Bible studies. They read their Bibles and prayed. What was holding them back from becoming true believers?

One day Pat asked me how Christians handle funerals. I realized she had asked the same question a few times over the past months. I suspected it was a barrier for her, but I didn't understand exactly what her issue was. I told her again, as I had on other occasions, that Christians know when we die our spirits go to be with God and what happens with our physical remains is of little consequence. Christians traditionally bury their dead, but we're okay with cremation as well. There are few cemeteries in Thailand since over 90 percent of the country is Buddhist, and Buddhists cremate their dead.

But Pat pushed the issue that day. She wanted to know the details of how Christians handle dead bodies from the time of death until they are buried or cremated.

I told her when a Thai Christian dies the family dresses the body in nice clothes and places it in a casket or on a table, depending on their economic status. They usually keep it in the living room for three days while friends and relatives spend time praying for and encouraging the family. Each day they serve food and conduct a funeral service with worship and preaching. After the final funeral service on the third day, they go to the cemetery together for a brief graveside service before the body is buried or cremated.

Pat seemed uncomfortable. I asked if she understood the part about the spirit leaving the body upon death and that the body is no longer a person. She assured me she understood that well. She knew the physical body would die and decay, and her spirit would live eternally with God.

She finally told me what was really bothering her. Her village was extremely concerned about funeral rituals. When a villager died, monks immediately got involved, washing and preparing the body according to specific guidelines. They chanted precise prayers. They divined the auspicious moment for cremation, placed the body in a beautiful casket, set it on a four-wheeled cart, and lined up monks and family members in a predetermined order to pull the cart to the crematorium with a long rope. Chanting monks and beating drums led the funeral procession, and when they reached the crematorium, they pulled the casket around it clockwise three times and then up the ramp to the cremation oven. Each funeral guest made a final visit to the casket, took a moment to *wai*, and dropped a small piece of tinder onto it. Then at a precise moment, the fire was lit.

The villagers believed if any part of this complicated ritual were botched or forgotten or simply didn't meet the approval of the deceased person, his or her spirit would be angry and cause havoc in the village. Storms, floods, fires, misunderstandings, hauntings, and all sorts of problems were attributed to offenses caused by funerals. The whole village stressed over every funeral, watching to make sure the deceased person's family and the monks were handling the body correctly.

Pat could easily imagine how the villagers would respond to her future death as a believer. They would watch the Christian funeral rituals in horror and terror! No monks would come to chant and bathe her body according to the sacred mandates. None of the critical funeral ceremonies or rites would happen. Christian worship and preaching would appear completely foreign. Her casket would be unceremoniously placed in the back of a pickup truck and hauled away to be buried somewhere the village didn't know about. Meanwhile, the villagers would be trembling in anticipation of the violent retribution Pat's ghost was about to bring down on them.

But that wasn't the worst part. Pat could live with all that. She knew it didn't matter what happened to her body after death. Her immortal spirit would leave her body and be united with Jesus. The part that troubled her was what would happen to her family and her Christian neighbors left behind. Every bad thing that happened in the village following her death—every storm, every disaster, every death, every accident—would be blamed on the Christians who had refused to conduct her funeral in the correct Buddhist way. They would be hated by the village. No one would buy or sell their produce. No one would watch over them like good neighbors are expected to do. Pat knew she couldn't protect her family and friends from the attack and rejection of the entire village if she died as a Christian.

Pat carried a massive weight of responsibility. She was the leader of this local group, and she began to wonder if she was leading them into misery. If she transitioned from *seeker* to *believer*, others would too, and they would surely suffer serious consequences. She didn't know what to do.

I didn't know what to tell her. No answers came to mind. The voice of the Holy Spirit was quiet this time. I wondered if I could come up with Christian funeral ceremonies to substitute for each Buddhist one, but I knew even if I came close to copying the rituals, they would never be accepted by the villagers, because I wouldn't be using the correct incantations. Besides, I wasn't a shaven-headed, orange-robed, ordained Buddhist monk. Even worse, I would run the risk of moving from *contextualization*[18] into *syncretism*.[19] Bad idea.

I prayed about the situation for weeks. The only thing I could think to tell Pat was that sometimes the cost of following Jesus was high, but her eternal life was at stake. She should step out, pay the price, and trust God to take care of her family after she died. But I couldn't bring myself to tell her those things. After all, she wasn't concerned about the cost to herself. She was concerned for her husband, her daughter, her infant grandson, and the neighbors who would follow her lead. This seemed like an impossible situation.

Then one day, thanks to the intercession of our faithful supporters, the most unexpected answer came straight from our loving, all-wise God.

Janie and I were visiting the small after-school center we had set up near Pat's house in Ban Pong village. Pat approached us with a huge smile on her face and told us about a woman from Ban Pong who had decided years ago to donate her body to Chiang Mai University for scientific study. The previous day the woman passed away, and her family had strict instructions to contact the university immediately upon her death. The family did so, and in a matter of hours, the university sent an ambulance to Ban Pong and took her body away. No one in the village reacted negatively. If anything, they admired the

18 *"Contextualization* attempts to communicate the Gospel in word and deed...in ways that make sense to people within their local cultural context." Darrell L. Whiteman, "Contextualization: The Theory, the Gap, the Challenge," *International Bulletin of Missionary Research*, January 1997, 2, http://www. internationalbulletin.org/issues/1997-01/1997-01-002-whiteman.pdf.
19 *Syncretism* means "the combining of different religions, cultures, or ideas." Cambridge Dictionary, s.v. "syncretism," accessed March 19, 2021, https:// dictionary.cambridge.org/us/dictionary/english/syncretism.

woman's willingness to contribute to scientific study.

Pat immediately knew what to do. That morning she got on her motorbike, drove to Chiang Mai University, found the science department, and filled out all the paperwork necessary to donate her body immediately upon her death. She was still excited about it when she reached us that afternoon. She had discovered a way to be a true, water-baptized believer without jeopardizing her family and neighbors when she died.

"How soon can I be water baptized?" she asked. She was ready!

A few days later, we baptized Pat in the swimming pool at the Juniper Tree Christian Resort just a few miles from Ban Pong village. It was a joyous, liberating, breakthrough day!

Several months later, Janie and I were working at the after-school center in Ban Pong again when Pat's husband Suchart approached me. With a big smile on his face, he said, "Guess what I did last evening."

"What?" I asked. I had no clue what he would say. He attended many of the Thursday evening Bible studies, but was often away working and still had a drinking problem he couldn't seem to overcome.

"I went to the university and donated my body," he said proudly. "Now I'm ready to get water baptized!"

Wow! The verdict was in! The pattern of becoming a Christian in Ban Pong was established: first, donate your body to Chiang Mai University. Only God could come up with an answer like that!

OVERCOMING BARRIERS TO SALVATION

For many people, deciding to become a genuine, committed follower of Christ is difficult. All of us know family members and friends who won't or can't take that step of faith. I have prayed for a certain relative's salvation for over 50 years, and he has yet to decide for Jesus.

Perhaps you have family members or friends in the same position. There are barriers standing in the way of their decision. At times, even they themselves may not know why they can't take a step of faith. But God knows what each barrier is. Pat's experience taught me there is no barrier too tall for Him! No matter what is blocking your friend or family member from giving his or her life to Jesus, God has the key to overcoming the barrier!

Discovering the key starts and ends with prayer. Pray, and don't give up (Luke 18:1-8)! I had no answer for Pat's barrier, but God answered our prayers and our supporters' prayers and provided a solution only He could contrive. Pray He will reveal the obstacles to your loved one's salvation and show you His solution to overcome them.

Instead of badgering or debating with your loved ones over the decision to follow Christ, simply be available to them. If they are willing to talk to you about God, they're probably already in the *seeker* category. That's good! Talk about the good things God has done for you, the prayers He's answered, the comfort He's given, the peace He places in your heart, and the love you have for Him.

Offer to pray over them. Be bold. I have observed that God answers prayers on behalf of the lost more frequently than for the found! God desires their salvation. Give Him a chance to display His power and love.

SPIRITUAL INSIGHTS & PRAYERS

When leading someone to a saving knowledge of Jesus, there is often one major stumbling block keeping him or her from taking a step of faith. For Sai it was her belief in her father's ghost. For Pat it was her funeral. Often we do not know what the barrier is, and we must rely on the Holy Spirit to reveal it. When we know what it is, we must pray until God reveals the solution. God knows how to remove barriers and release people to welcome Jesus into their lives.

PRAY FOR BUDDHISTS

I pray for Buddhists who are interested in following Christ but have barriers preventing them from taking that step. God, reveal the barriers and make a way to overcome them and follow You.

PRAY FOR MISSIONARIES

I pray missionaries and Christian workers will be sensitive to Your voice to recognize key barriers that hold Buddhists back from salvation. Give them wisdom and anointing to help Buddhists overcome those barriers and follow You.

PRAY FOR YOURSELF

I pray for my relatives and friends who are not believers. Reveal the barriers that stand in the way of their salvation. I confront those barriers in Your name and ask for wisdom to know what to do to help my loved ones overcome them and receive salvation.

CHAPTER EIGHT
BAPTISM OR MONKHOOD?

For most Thais, the path from Buddhist to Christian is long and slow. These worldviews are on opposite ends of the spectrum, and the journey towards mature Christianity is filled with obstacles that create misunderstandings about who God is, who humans are, why we exist, what godliness is, how to behave, how to relate to others, and a plethora of other questions. Almost without exception, the successful navigation of that path requires a faithful guide—a discipler. I quickly learned discipleship and evangelism must happen simultaneously. Discipleship starts as soon as the unreached person is curious about God. In fact, I am much less interested in obtaining someone's commitment to be born again than his or her commitment to learn about God. I know when someone learns who God is and what He did to save them, the commitment will be made voluntarily. Fairly early on in my missionary career in Thailand, I set a goal to have at least one personal discipling relationship going on at all times. Prin was one of those disciples.

PRIN PHETPRAPHAI

I met Prin the beginning of his senior year at Rajamongkhon Institute of Technology in Chiang Mai. Prin was an artist and athlete majoring in ceramic art and starting on the men's basketball team. Like most Thai students, Prin wanted to improve his English, so he joined a conversational English group at an outreach center where Janie and I served during some of our early years in Thailand. When I found out he was a basketball player, I invited him to join me and a group of missionaries who played twice a week. He did so, and that was the start of a friendship that continues to this day.

God ordained my friendship with Prin. He was spiritually open to Jesus, he needed friends, he needed a father figure, and he loved basketball. We were the perfect match. I wish there were an evangelistic algorithm that could match up Christians with like-minded people who need the gospel. It would make us incredibly effective in reaching people for Christ.

Our friendship required a measure of planning too. Strategy definitely has a place in missions. Janie and I went to Thailand with a plan to focus on university students, because they tend to be more open-minded and receptive to the gospel than the general populace, and because they will eventually become the leaders and influencers in their nations. It was a solid plan, and it produced good results, but when Janie and I look back over our nearly 30 years in Thailand, the most effective, valuable things we did were not planned. I should say, they were not planned by *us*, although they were certainly planned by God. Ministry must be strategic, but more importantly, it must be led by the Holy Spirit.

As I reflect on Prin's discipleship experience, he was probably the quickest and easiest Buddhist *seeker* convert I ever knew. At the first invitation, he started attending TLC Church on Sunday mornings, which is not normal for most Thai college students. Nearly all of them consider Christianity to be a religion of foreigners that has nothing to do with their lives. But Prin loved music and enjoyed the TLC worship team's upbeat songs. He loved the company of the young people and respected the pastor and church leaders. He was hundreds of miles away from home, and the church quickly became his new family. He was open and receptive to Jesus.

I don't remember the moment Prin prayed the sinner's prayer, but it happened pretty quickly. Within a matter of weeks, he began to identify as a Christian. He attended church faithfully and soon was invited to join the worship team as one of the guitarists.

It might have been Prin's first Sunday morning at TLC when I asked him if he would like to study Christianity with me once a week. To my great joy he said yes! Every Tuesday morning we met at the church to study what it means to commit one's life to Jesus. We examined the character of God, the life of Jesus, prayer, Bible reading and study, the Church, and many other basic Christian concepts. Prin was eager to learn these strange new beliefs and was quick to apply them to his life. He practiced regular morning prayer and Bible reading, memorized Scripture, and learned worship songs. He was a star disciple!

Some months into our Tuesday morning Bible studies, we focused for three weeks on water baptism, examining Romans 6 and other relevant passages. After our comprehensive study, during which Prin was interested and interactive, I asked him the big question: "Prin, would you like to be baptized in water?"

His answer floored me. "I have been thinking hard about this for the past three weeks and am not sure what I should do," he answered. "I have not yet fulfilled my duty to *buatpenphra*." I could hardly believe my ears! Prin still wanted to fulfill his duty to become a Buddhist monk!

He went on to explain he felt obligated to his mother to become a monk immediately after graduation in a few months, remain a monk for the minimum three-day requirement, and then be done with it. He suspected there might be a spiritual conflict if he were to get water baptized now and become a monk a few months later. He wondered aloud if it would be better to wait to be baptized until after he completed his obligation.

I felt like a failure as a discipler. How could Prin not understand that becoming a Buddhist monk—even for just three days—was the last thing a Christian should consider doing? Didn't he understand he had aligned himself with Jesus and separated himself from Buddhism? Or perhaps he thought becoming a monk was a harmless custom?

I took a deep breath and tried to hide my disappointment. In a calm voice, I asked why he felt the need to become a monk. His answer opened my eyes to some of the pressure-filled expectations placed on young Buddhist men in Thai society.

Prin's mother, like all Buddhist women, could not hope to attain *nirvana* as a female. A woman must make every effort to do good deeds, live a good life, and make merit throughout her lifetime in hopes of being reborn as a man. In Thailand a woman cannot become a monk—Buddhism's maximum merit-making activity—but her son may one day become a monk and endow her with the highest form of merit possible for a woman, allowing her to be reborn as a man and placing her in a position to attain *nirvana*.

When Prin was born, his mother viewed him as her salvation. He would one day become a monk and provide her with enough merit to potentially result in a better rebirth. In her mind, the quality of her next life rested largely on his shoulders. Before he became a Christian, Prin had been proud to accept that responsibility and was determined not to let his mother down. It was one of his central purposes in life. But becoming a believer left him confused. Becoming a monk would result in his mother's salvation, at least in his old way of thinking, but it was incongruent with his commitment to Jesus Christ.

Water baptism would be his public declaration of a lifetime of commitment to Jesus, but becoming a monk included a vow to "take refuge" in the Three Jewels, saying, "I take refuge in the Buddha. I take refuge in the *dharma* [the teachings of Buddha]. I take refuge in the *sangha* [the monastic order]." Prin understood clearly that becoming an ordained monk would clash with water baptism, but he loved his mother and could not imagine letting her down after 20 years of anticipation.

After Prin explained all this to me, I began to understand the tremendous weight of his mom's expectations. I wondered how to respond. Should I challenge him to take a decisive stand and tell his mother he now belonged to Jesus and could not submit himself to monkhood? Or should I simply pray for him and wait for the Holy Spirit to prepare him to take that stand? It was obvious he didn't fully understand what it meant to place himself under Christ's lordship. But what if he went ahead with becoming a monk? What spiritual dangers would he risk by participating in Buddhist ceremonies and three days of training in the temple?

I prayed for wisdom and the leading of the Holy Spirit. I'm certain someone was praying for me as an idea leapt into my thoughts. The words flowed from my mouth before I could think about what I was going to say. I asked Prin if we could pray that his mother would meet Jesus and become a believer before he graduated. If she became a Christian, she would no longer expect him to become a Buddhist monk. Prin looked surprised. That idea had not occurred to him. Relief crossed his face, and he agreed to pray.

Every week we asked the Lord to open doors for Prin's mother to hear the gospel and give her heart to Jesus. She came to visit a few weeks later, and Janie and I were able to talk with her about Jesus. She attended TLC Church with us and met Prin's new church family. She seemed to accept and love us all. Before she returned home, she asked Janie and me to take care of her son as if he were our own. We prayed for her and sent her on her way. Her heart was open to Jesus, but without a group of Christians around her, she had no idea how to conceptualize what living as a Christian meant. We tried to connect her with a church in her area to no avail.

Several weeks before the end of the school year, Prin asked to talk to me about something very important. TLC was planning a water baptism service in the next week or so, and Prin announced he would like to get baptized.

"What about your commitment to becoming a monk?" I asked him. "Are you still planning on following through with that?"

"No," said Prin with an intense look on his face. "I am ready to tell my mom that becoming a monk will not save her or help her in another rebirth. I am ready to tell her Jesus alone can help her, and the best way I can show her I love her is by not becoming a monk."

I teared up. Prin's decision was incredibly difficult. His mother would not understand why he refused to follow through with what she considered a simple ceremony to ensure her hope of a better rebirth. His refusal might cause her to question his love for her. But his decision demonstrated he truly understood Jesus' call to leave everything and follow Him.

Prin's mom seemed to take the news in stride, and he was baptized. He went on to study at YWAM's School of Worship and became TLC's worship leader for several years before getting married and moving to Ireland. Prin also became a discipler of others. One of the young men he discipled is the current worship leader at TLC. Prin understood that one-on-one discipleship is necessary to help new believers overcome the many obstacles standing in the way of genuine commitment to Christ and growth to maturity.

I asked Prin for permission to include his story. After reading this section, he told me he had never considered my perspective on the day he told me about his struggle between baptism and monkhood. He didn't realize I felt disheartened over his lack of spiritual understanding. I had hidden my disappointment well. He believes if I had reacted negatively to his desire to become a monk or told him he must not do the ceremony, he would

My response did not come from my own wisdom or experience. It came from the leading of the Holy Spirit, and I am convinced someone was praying for me.

probably have rejected Christianity and would not be a believer today. My gentle response and invitation to pray for his mom were exactly what he needed. Believe me, my response did not come from my own wisdom or experience. It came from the leading of the Holy Spirit, and I am convinced it came because someone was praying for me.

WAT WONGWAD

"Discipleship isn't complete until reproduction takes place." That's a slogan I've used many times teaching discipleship in various settings over the years. My pastor and mentor from the 1970s and 80s, Dr. James Bradford, used to say discipleship is, "Second Timothy 2:2-ing it to the world." That verse says, "What you have heard from me in the presence of many witnesses entrust to faithful men, who will be able to teach others also." Paul taught it, Timothy heard it and passed it on to faithful men and women, and they taught others. Discipleship means passing spiritual understanding to people who will do the same.

But even after a disciple reproduces themselves by making another disciple, the original discipleship relationship should continue. The relationship might evolve into a mentoring relationship or a friendship, but genuine relationships continue for a lifetime. Prin and I are still friends, and he sometimes contacts me for counsel, just as I sometimes contact Dr. Bradford for counsel. Wat Wongwad is another disciple I kept working with long after his initial discipleship process.

Wat was a new believer when I arrived in Chiang Mai but was already actively involved as a student leader at Nakhorn Ping Church, where we helped during our first two years in Thailand. Wat was an engineering student at Chiang Mai University. He was a natural leader, respected and admired by his peers. Because Janie and I hosted weekly university student meetings at our home, we got to know Wat well during his final years at CMU.

The night of Wat's graduation, we hosted a party for him and a few other graduates at our home. Toward the end of the evening, we prayed that God would guide each of the graduate's next steps. While we were praying for Wat, Janie sensed the Holy Spirit telling her that Wat was called to pastoral ministry. He acknowledged as much when she spoke with him, but he didn't seem excited about it. Later we found out he had a misinformed belief that a call to pastoral ministry meant sacrificing all his possessions to live in abject poverty. As a top engineering graduate at a prestigious university, Wat was not excited about submitting to that kind of call.

Within days of graduating, Wat told Janie and me that his parents were taking him to the beaches of southern Thailand to celebrate. Weeks went by, and he still hadn't returned. We heard rumors he had taken a job in Bangkok, 400 miles south of Chiang Mai. When I finally connected with him by phone, Wat sounded rather sheepish and reported he had found an engineering job in Bangkok. He knew God called him into the ministry, but he believed he was called to evangelize and disciple his engineering colleagues. I was supportive, but my prophetic wife was unhappy. In fact, she began to earnestly intercede for Wat out of a sense of grief that he was missing God's call.

Nearly a year passed, and we rarely heard from Wat. Then one day he called me and began to release pent-up emotions. He felt miserable, not physically but emotionally and spiritually. He thought he could fulfill God's call by sharing the gospel with his coworkers, but it wasn't enough. He knew there was much more he was supposed to do. He had a hunger to preach, teach, disciple, and minister to the people of God. Wow! Janie was right (of course).

Wat was called into pastoral ministry, but a huge obstacle stood in his way: obligation to his parents. They had raised Wat and his siblings in the small town of Chai Prakan near the Thai-Myanmar border. By running a small household goods store and farming a small piece of land, his parents were able to raise enough money to send Wat to Chiang Mai to finish high school and pay for his entire university education. As the eldest son, Wat was expected to get a lucrative job and support his parents for the rest of their lives. It is normal in Thai culture for children to be the primary social security system. They are obligated by culture to take care of their parents from retirement to death. Because Wat was smart, gifted, and well-educated, the expectations on him were high.

To make matters worse, Wat's father had drinking and gambling problems and was carrying a debt of 3 million baht (approximately $120,000 USD at the time). Debtors were threatening to confiscate their property, which had been in the family for many generations. The family was keeping this a secret from Grandma, who lived with them, because she was old and in poor health. They feared if she found out about the threat to the family property, she would die of a broken heart. They were counting on Wat to pay off the debt, protect the property, and save Grandma's life.

"What should I do?" Wat asked me over the phone.

I needed Holy Spirit wisdom! I hoped someone was praying for me at that moment.

I told Wat he must pray, pray, and pray some more. I could not tell him what to do, but if he listened, he would hear the voice of the Holy Spirit leading him. I would pray for him to clearly sense God's leading and support whatever decision he made. There was a line I knew I should not cross. Wat needed to know for certain that his decision came from the Holy Spirit, not Mark Durene.

Over the next few months, Wat called me several times, still miserable. He was not fulfilling God's call to full-time ministry and didn't know how to balance the call with his moral obligation to his family. To further complicate the decision, his pastor said he had a scriptural obligation to honor, obey, and provide for his family and should continue working as an engineer until his father's debt was paid off.

During a trip to Bangkok, I took the opportunity to talk and pray with Wat about his decision. We tried to figure out how long it would take to come up with 3 million baht, and as we spoke the Holy Spirit gave him a powerful revelation I clearly remember to this day. Wat suddenly realized that even if God miraculously supplied funds to pay off the debt, the financial miracle would still not be enough to lead his parents and siblings to faith in Jesus. He knew his best chance to reach his parents was resigning his job, apologizing for his inability to take care of them financially, and explaining how his obligation to God was higher than his obligation to his family. Wat was emotionally shaken at his decision but determined to follow through.

The cost of serving Jesus in Thailand and other Buddhist countries is astronomical. It took several months, but Wat was ready to pay the price. Weeks later I received a phone call from him.

"Guess what I just did," he said. "I resigned my job."

I choked up. He was willing to pay a high price to obey God's call. I asked about his next step and wasn't quite ready for the answer.

"I'm moving back to Chiang Mai to prepare for full-time ministry," he said.

"Where will you study? Where will you live?"

"I'm moving in with you," Wat responded. "I want you to teach me how to be a pastor."

I probably stammered. I had a wife and three kids. I knew the kids wouldn't be comfortable adding someone to our household. I wasn't sure what Janie would say, although she was the one who told him he was called into full-time ministry. But what could I say?

"You're most welcome," I told him. Two weeks later we had a houseguest.

Wat lived with us for about six months. Janie taught him English, I gave him reading assignments, and he followed me around in all my ministry responsibilities. We dreamed about planting a new church next to Chiang Mai University. However, since our first furlough was approaching, we decided to send him back to Bangkok to study for his Master of Divinity at Bangkok Bible Seminary and intern at Bangkok Liberty Church. Upon our return to Thailand, he would move back to Chiang Mai, and we would plant a new church together.

It took three years, but finally Wat moved back to Chiang Mai with an M.Div. and a wife. Nuu was the perfect companion for him with her musical talent, creative abilities, love for ministry, and best of all, her passion for Jesus. The two of them moved into our house, and it was the delight of our ministry career to dream, pray, plan, and work together planting Chiang Mai Liberty Church over the coming months.

CLC grew slowly at first but is now a thriving church that has already planted a daughter church with goals of planting many more. I couldn't be prouder of Wat and Nuu!

As with Prin, Wat and I both needed Holy Spirit guidance during critical moments in our discipling relationship. Our intercessors' prayers were working to open my ears to God's leading and to guide Wat's decisions. They held the staff high, so the swords in our hands would be victorious.

SUCCESSFUL DISCIPLESHIP PRINCIPLES

QUALITY RELATIONSHIP

Quality discipleship demands a quality relationship. Prin would not have explained his mother's expectations if he did not trust me and feel close to me. Wat would not have revealed his family's debt if we had not built a strong relationship. Our quality relationships did not come primarily from my spiritual insights but from playing basketball, visiting at our home, going out to eat, hanging out at church, and meeting one another's families. Building a quality relationship outside formal training time is critical to a successful discipleship relationship.

HOLY SPIRIT DIRECTION

I've made it a practice to actively disciple at least one person at all times. Identifying a disciple starts with prayer. I ask the Holy Spirit to direct me to a potential world-changer who is eager to learn and grow in their faith. I didn't always get world-changers, but I believe God led me to people He wanted me to invest in each time. Ask God to lead you to someone hungry for spiritual maturity.

PATIENCE

Maybe things happen more slowly in Thailand than in other places, but it sometimes takes years to guide a disciple to spiritual maturity. Prin and Wat grew relatively quickly, but I have discipled men who never got there and ultimately walked away from the faith. You may question whether I was Spirit-led in those cases, but I believe the investment was worth the effort despite the loss in the end. Patience usually pays off. Yeah (that's his name—"Yeah") is an example of someone who finally came through after many years of investment. He attended English classes and spent time with Christians for more than 10 years before finally giving his life to Jesus. Hang in there! Eventually your investment in lives will bring great rewards.

PRAYER

Praying *before* starting a meeting with one's disciple is absolutely necessary, but I've found that praying together *during* the meeting provides an opportunity for the Holy Spirit to convict of sin, seal spiritual principles, transform thoughts, reveal insights, and supercharge the maturation process. Take time to pray with your disciple before, after, and even during teaching times.

THE WORD

Hebrews 4:12 tells us God's Word is like a sharp, two-edged sword "discerning the thoughts and intentions of the heart." Make sure the Bible is central to your discipleship meetings. Scripture is alive, poised to leap off the pages to inspire amazing insights and reveal astounding truths. When I bring those expectations into discipleship encounters, studying Scripture is never boring. Show excitement about studying God's Word, and your meetings will be filled with life. Carry the same enthusiasm into memorizing and quoting Scripture to elevate the significance of the Bible to your disciple.

CURRICULUM

I have learned that studying the "right" curriculum has far less impact than simply getting together on a regular basis. However, that doesn't mean curriculum is unimportant. Look for good material, but don't search for a magic curriculum that will transform your disciple's life. Your *relationship* will be transformational. Use curriculum to launch discussions about real issues, and ask the Holy Spirit for wisdom to negotiate those issues with your disciple.

GIFTS OF THE SPIRIT

A defining moment in my men's small group happened through the gifts of the Holy Spirit. Thirty minutes before the five guys in my group were to arrive, I was looking through my notes and praying for each person one-by-one. As I prayed for the first guy, a specific prophetic word for him leapt into my mind. I wrote it down, excited to share it with him when he arrived. This was not normal for me, so I knew sharing it would be a special moment.

Then I began praying for the next guy. Lo and behold, a prophetic word for him came, and I wrote it down. You guessed it; the same thing happened for all five men.

When they arrived, I could hardly wait to tell them what happened. One by one I shared prophetic words specific to each of them. It was an emotional and sacred time together that impacted their hearts and had a side benefit as well—it changed the way they viewed me as their leader. They knew for sure I prayed for them and was concerned about their spiritual well-being. I became a much stronger spiritual influence in their lives from that day forward.

Be intentional about using spiritual gifts in discipleship. Ask the Holy Spirit to speak through you to touch the deepest part of your disciples' lives through words of wisdom, words of knowledge, faith, healing, miracles, prophecy, discernment, tongues, and interpretation (1 Corinthians 12:8-10).

The Holy Spirit wants to transform people and knows how to do it far better than you or I. Let's give Him a chance to do so!

REPRODUCTION

Discipleship is not complete until reproduction happens. Early in the discipleship process, encourage your disciples to begin passing on the things they learn. One of the benefits of using a curriculum is that the disciples take home

Scripture is alive, poised to leap off the pages to inspire amazing insights and reveal astounding truths. When I bring those expectations into discipleship encounters, studying Scripture is never boring.

material they can use with someone else. Try to keep the end goal of reproduction in mind throughout the process. It will help you teach in a replicable way. Then guide them into discipling roles with others, and pray they will continue to make new disciples all their lives.

Every time someone asks about the biggest accomplishments in my ministry career (excluding my kids), the answer comes without hesitation: Prin, Wat, Apple, King, Pat, and others whose lives we invested in, who are now bearing fruit for Jesus. There is no higher ministry calling than to invest in people. They're all we can bring to heaven with us. Churches, Bible schools, books, curriculum, and accomplishments will not make it through the pearly gates, but the souls we invested in will be there. I can't wait!

SPIRITUAL INSIGHTS & PRAYERS

Regardless of one's religious background, discipleship is crucial for new believers, especially Buddhist-background believers. Effective discipleship happens in the context of a personal relationship between a disciple and a discipler who are interacting together under the Holy Spirit's supernatural guidance. This discipleship process is not complete until reproduction takes place.

PRAY FOR BUDDHISTS

I pray Buddhist-background seekers and new believers will become strongly connected with mature believers who will disciple them patiently and accurately for as long as it takes to become reproducing disciplers. Through discipleship, the Scriptures, and Your guidance, transform them into strong, solid, unshakable followers of Jesus Christ.

PRAY FOR MISSIONARIES

I pray missionaries and Christian workers will be eager and prepared to disciple Buddhist-background seekers and new believers. Anoint them to exercise the gifts of the Holy Spirit as they guide their disciples into maturity in Christ.

PRAY FOR YOURSELF

Holy Spirit, use me to disciple someone. May my life and words encourage, strengthen, guide, and mentor younger believers to love You with all their hearts, souls, minds, and strength.

CHAPTER NINE
A DAUGHTER OF WITCH DOCTORS

TLC Church experienced a period of rapid growth in its first two years thanks to a number of dramatic miracles: Pastor Thaweesak's knee was healed, cataracts evaporated from Noi's eyes, and Jiw's cancer vanished. The miracles attracted people, demonstrated God's presence and power, and resulted in many first-time converts. In 24 months, the church grew to over 100. It was truly exciting!

During the growth period, water baptisms were happening regularly. Baptism candidates were required to take a two- or three-week new convert class to make sure they understood what it meant to be Christians and to prepare them for their ceremonial public profession of their lifetime commitment to follow Jesus.

A young woman we will call Jam was among those who committed her life to Jesus. She attended the classes and was baptized in water. A week later, Jam came to me after Sunday morning service to ask for prayer, because an evil spirit had been hassling her all week. The day after her baptism, she stepped out of the front door of her parents' home and was startled to see a woman standing on the edge of the roof of the building across the street. As Jam watched in horror, the woman jumped off the building! However, the moment she hit the ground, she vanished! Jam recognized immediately this was an evil spirit who was displeased with her decision to follow Christ and was warning her to give it up.

Jam would not have made a big deal about the incident except wherever she went throughout the week, this spirit appeared in front of her, jumping off tall buildings. In fact, it had happened across the street from the church when she arrived earlier that morning. She asked that we pray the spirit would stop harassing her.

As I write this, I am reminded how much Thailand's spiritual worldview has changed me. If someone had come to me with this story during the years I pastored in Minnesota, I most likely would have questioned his or her sanity. But that question did not even occur to me. The believers around me and I simply accepted Jam's story that an evil spirit was trying to scare her out of her salvation. Satan and his forces rarely reveal themselves that way in America—perhaps because the Western worldview gives little credence to demonic appearances— but this kind of thing is not unusual in Thailand.

I asked the people standing around Jam and me to pray together for her. But first I asked if she was still fully committed to following Jesus and submitting to His lordship. She answered strongly in the affirmative. I asked if there was sin or anything else in her life that might open the door for Satan. She didn't think so. Finally, I asked if she had idols or amulets—in her home, on her motorbike, or on her person—that she was trusting for protection, security, or good luck. Her answer took me aback. "Lots of them," she said.

Jam explained her parents were professional fortune-telling spirit doctors. Her parents had taught her to read palms as a child, and her skill turned out to be excellent for business. Reading palms was second nature to her. Even though she knew as a Christian it was wrong, she couldn't help but look at people's hands—even mine. I felt like putting my hands in my pockets.

Since Jam still lived with her parents, I knew she couldn't destroy all their household idols, so I tried the second-best option. I asked if she had her own bedroom or at least her own space set apart in her parents' house. Yes, she had her own bedroom. I asked if she would remove all the idols from her room, and we would dedicate it to Jesus as His own set-apart place and pray for God's dome of protection to surround her there.

Jam paused and pondered for a moment. She was counting the cost, and it was much higher than I imagined. She told us her parents had given her an idol or amulet for every birthday, every holiday, and every auspicious occasion since she was a kid. Her room was filled with hundreds of idols worth mounds of money. Financial considerations, spiritual bonds, and relational obligations were working together to form a huge barrier to her faith in Christ. She couldn't imagine throwing all that away. She finally said she didn't think she could do it.

With increasing urgency I explained that each idol represented a spiritual force with a measure of influence or authority over her life, and unless she renounced their influence and removed them from her space, she would not be free from the spirit that was harassing her. I offered to explain to her parents what was happening and ask them to take the idols and amulets back. Jam understood the issues and agreed with me, but ultimately she confirmed again that she could not bring herself to part with them.

Thinking back on it, I don't know if the greatest impediment was her parents' feelings or the high monetary and spiritual value of the idols, but she couldn't bring herself to get rid of them.

We prayed for Jam anyway, asking the Holy Spirit to reveal His power and authority over the spiritual realm and give her courage to cut off the influence of demonic forces and surrender completely to God. She walked away in sadness—just like the rich young ruler Jesus encountered (Matthew 19:16-22; Mark 10:17-22; Luke 18:18-23). She knew it would cost her relationship with Jesus, but she wasn't ready to give up her expensive heap of treasures.

As far as I know, Jam never returned to Jesus. However, one Sunday several months later, she showed up at church with a friend having spiritual issues. Jam knew Jesus was her answer. She asked us to pray for her friend and hoped she would turn her life over to Jesus. Jam knew He had power over sin and Satan, but she was still not willing to give up her treasures to follow Him.

Satan fights hard to keep people from placing their whole lives in Jesus' hands and under His lordship. He can tolerate churchgoers as long as they hang on to their former gods. Because Jam's room was filled with gods she

> *Cultivating Christ's lordship requires the constant repetition of our commitment to declare God as the Lord over all thoughts, attitudes, words, deeds, motives, relationships, and plans. It means regularly acknowledging we are not the owners of our lives.*

couldn't part with, Satan had access into her life. In the same way, he has access to Christians whose rooms are filled with finances they won't place under Jesus' lordship, relationships they know are not pleasing to God, habits they don't want to break, and lifestyles that are contrary to Scripture. But when believers submit their complete selves to God's lordship, a spiritual battle begins to rage. Satan's battle strategy in spirit-conscious Thailand tends to involve obvious scare tactics like demons jumping off buildings. In America his strategy may be much more subtle, but he will fight just as hard to prevent believers from making Jesus their Lord.

Satan's battle against the lordship of Christ is not limited to new believers. If the most mature believers become unwilling to submit part of their lives to God's leadership, their relationships with God suffer, their spiritual lives weaken, their fruitfulness decreases, and their vulnerability to spiritual attack and sin grows. Peter challenges believers to "be sober-minded; be watchful. Your adversary the devil prowls around like a roaring lion, seeking someone to devour" (1 Peter 5:8).

Cultivating Christ's lordship requires the constant repetition of our commitment to declare God as the Lord over all thoughts, attitudes, words, deeds, motives, relationships, and plans. It means allowing the Holy Spirit to search our hearts to convict us of things that begin to take precedence over God. It means identifying temptations and deliberately placing them under God's authority. It means regularly acknowledging we are not the owners of our lives.

> *Do you not know that your body is a temple of the Holy Spirit within you, whom you have from God? You are not your own, for you were bought with a price. So glorify God in your body. (1 Corinthians 6:19-20)*

DEMONIC POSSESSION AND A CLOCK

Many Thais and Americans share Jam's unwillingness to break demonic connections and make Jesus their Savior and Lord. Her story would have been vastly different had she allowed us to go with her to talk to her parents about moving the idols out of her room. We would have prayed with her and renounced all ties with idols, spirits, palm reading, and any other spiritual strongholds. We would have commanded demonic spirits to leave her room. We would have dedicated her room to Jesus and asked for His protective dome to surround her. But Jam couldn't bring herself to cut the ties.

Pim's story is happier. She didn't have dozens of idols to renounce, but she did have a clock.

Pim and her husband Bay (not their real names) were new believers, and New Tribes Mission's language school hired her to provide daycare for children while their parents were studying Thai. They set her up in a small room next to the school. Our youngest daughter Jocelyn was not yet old enough for kindergarten, so we left her with Pim every day from 8 a.m. to noon while we studied. Little did we know that Pim was being harassed by demons the entire time.

One day Bay asked for a few minutes of my time. He told me Pim was being bothered by demons, especially at night. When the demon manifested, Pim would growl, bite, and threaten him.

It just so happened we were gathering for special prayer meetings that week, so I invited Bay and Pim to join me. All was calm until praise and worship started. On multiple occasions I have observed demonic activity during worship; I can only conclude they don't like it. The demons harassing Pim certainly didn't.

Bay nudged me. "It's happening," he said.

Pim was standing between us. I looked down at her, and she began writhing and growling like an animal. I grabbed one of her arms, and Bay grabbed the other. She tried to bite me.

I decided to get her out of the worship service, so we could pray with her in private. We pulled and dragged her to a back stairway and stopped on the first landing. After we rebuked the demonic spirits for an hour or so, Pim began to vomit and then settled down enough to begin responding to me. I asked if she possessed idols or amulets. She didn't. I asked about involvement with witch doctors and fortune tellers. She answered, "None." I asked if she had unconfessed sin in her life, and she responded that she couldn't think of any. I asked if Jesus was her Savior and Lord, and she answered, "Yes." I led her in a prayer of recommitment to Jesus, confessing Him as Savior and Lord. She went away better, but I believed there was still some unfinished business within her.

Several days later, Bay came to me with concern. He had woken up in the middle of the night with Pim standing over him, holding a large knife and making growling noises. He escaped, and Pim quickly settled down, but he feared for his life. He asked me to join his pastor and several other local ministers in a prayer meeting for Pim. It turned into an epic experience.

The prayer meeting took place late one evening in the auditorium of a small, simple church in Chiang Mai. All the plastic chairs were cleared and stacked against the outside walls. Pim, Bay, five Thai ministers, and I were the only ones there. Our agenda was to free Pim from the demonic influences hounding her, and she came willing and ready to submit to our prayers.

One of the Thai ministers took the lead. He asked Pim to reaffirm her commitment to Jesus as her Savior and Lord. She did so. Then we all surrounded her, laid hands on her, and began to pray. Immediately she began to growl, scratch, and bite at us. Bay helped force her to her knees, and for the next several hours we prayed, rebuked the devil, quoted

Scripture, and did all we could to cast out the demons. Nothing worked. Pim was still growling and fighting.

During the battle, the lead Thai minister repeatedly asked Pim what gave demonic spirits the right to harass her. At roughly 2 a.m., after several hours of laborious prayer, Pim finally responded to his repeated question.

"A clock," she said.

A clock? It was a strange response. But as hard as we tried to get more information, that's all she would say.

At first Bay was as confused as the rest of us, but then a thought occurred to him. He remembered that a few months back, during one of the Buddhist holidays, they went to the local temple grounds where a rummage sale of sorts was taking place. The items being sold were "blessed" by the temple monks so those who purchased them would have good luck and protection against evil spirits.

Buying things from temples is a form of merit-making, and Pim and Bay bought a clock and a large wall calendar. Like many Thai Christians, they believed making merit and procuring good luck objects didn't hurt anything. This time it did!

We knew what we had to do. We sent Bay home to get the clock and calendar. The pastor went to the church kitchen to get the clay oven, which looks like a medium-sized plant pot made with extra-thick sides. A grill is placed on top of the pot, and charcoal is burned inside to barbeque meat or heat cooking pots and pans. The church floor was cement, so we set the clay oven in the middle of the floor and lit it. Like most small churches in Thailand, this one had lots of windows, so we swung them wide open to vent the smoke from the open fire.

By the time Bay returned with the clock and calendar, the fire was hot. We tore the calendar into smaller pieces and burned it first. Pim knelt and watched it burn. Then we put the clock on the fire. It was a small wall clock made mostly of plastic. When it burned, thick, black, acrid smoke poured upward and began to fill the room. Pim was quiet. We all watched the clock melt into a black blob.

After a few moments of silence, we turned back to Pim. The atmosphere was amazingly calm. The pastor rebuked the demons and commanded them to leave in Jesus' name. Immediately a powerful peace flooded the room and was reflected in Pim's countenance. It was over. The demonic spirits were gone. Pim was free.

A few years later, Pim and Bay finished Bible school and began to serve as lead pastors in a small church in Chiang Mai. The demonic spirits never returned to bother her.

Immediately a powerful peace flooded the room and was reflected in Pim's countenance. It was over. The demonic spirits were gone. Pim was free. The demonic spirits never returned to bother her.

My demonology isn't formed on the foundation of experiences such as those with Jam's idols and Pim's clock, but those experiences illustrate the following principles about the nature of demons and demonic influence. I am using the word "influence," because there isn't time or space in these pages to debate the "possession" versus "oppression" question. Suffice it to say, I do believe Christians are vulnerable to demonic influence if they are not careful to make Jesus their only God and Lord.

LORDSHIP

God must be the only spiritual power in a believer's life. When someone places his or her trust in an idol or good luck charm, God is no longer the sole spiritual authority. Both Jam and Pim possessed idols and charms that represented help and security coming from something other than God. When God is the Lord of our lives, no other being or object exerts spiritual influence over us.

Spiritual freedom only comes after one acknowledges Jesus as Lord, renounces spiritual powers other than God, and removes objects—physical, conceptual, or spiritual—from one's life.

DEMONIC INFLUENCE

If a believer allows an object, whether material or spiritual, to share God's place as the sole provider, a dangerous door of demonic influence can open in that believer's life. Both Jam and Pim held on to things that allowed demonic influence to have a foothold.

RENOUNCE AND REMOVE

Spiritual freedom only comes after one acknowledges Jesus as Lord, renounces spiritual powers other than God, and removes objects— physical, conceptual, or spiritual—from one's life. Renouncing and removing are physical acts that demonstrate and confirm one's faith. Pim was willing to remove her clock and was freed from demonic influence. Jam was unwilling to remove her idols and lost her faith, just like the rich young ruler who was unwilling to give up his possessions and follow Jesus.

CHOICE

The human will is powerful. God created us with the ability to choose whether or not we will submit to Him. When demonically influenced people refuse to give up spiritual objects or ideas, it is difficult, if not impossible, to cast demons out of them. Jam made a conscious decision to keep her idols, and as long as she was unwilling to give them up, her eternal destiny was doomed. When Pim finally realized the clock was the source of her spiritual bondage, she willingly gave it up and received her freedom.

GOD'S HIERARCHY

Demonic spirits are nothing to be trifled with. However, Scripture teaches that believers have authority over them. Jesus gave that authority to His disciples for a special outreach in Luke 9:1. In His Great Commission, Jesus said casting out demons would be a sign accompanying belief in Him (Mark 16:17). Through God's power, believers are equipped to cast out demonic spirits.

Remember our discussion in Chapter Three about God's created order? Human beings are the elite of God's creation. Nothing is higher in all the universe. Not even the angels rank above human beings. We are not to pray to or worship angels, because they are not created for that role. It is no wonder Jesus gives us authority to cast out demons. Lucifer, our ultimate spiritual enemy and leader of the demonic realm, is a fallen angel. He is incredibly powerful, but by nature he is a created being who is lower than you and me in God's hierarchy! All demons are in that category.

I must include an important caution here. In this era of fallen humanity, we are completely and entirely dependent on the presence of the Holy Spirit to exercise authority over demons. Our power over demons does not come from the fact that we are above them in God's created order, but from the power of God working through us.

We must maintain daily relationship with God and foster the presence and power of the Holy Spirit in our lives. As Spirit-filled believers, it is incredibly encouraging to know God's power at work in us places Satan and his legions "under our feet" (Romans 16:20). As long as the Holy Spirit dwells in us, we need not fear the demonic realm.

SPIRITUAL INSIGHTS & PRAYERS

Spiritual freedom can be challenging for believers with histories of demonic involvement. They must be willing to renounce all ungodly spiritual alliances and remove related objects—physical, conceptual, or spiritual—from their lives to maintain freedom from demonic influence. Most Eastern Buddhists live in cultures where demonic involvement is common. New believers coming out of those cultures need our prayers for their spiritual freedom.

PRAY FOR BUDDHISTS

I pray for Buddhist-background believers who were saved from demonic involvement. May they be bold to renounce and remove all demonic influences. Let Your dome of protection cover them and provide complete spiritual freedom.

PRAY FOR MISSIONARIES

I pray for a special anointing to fall on missionaries and Christian workers to discern and rebuke demonic influences at work in the lives of new Buddhist-background believers. Equip them spiritually, and make them ready to stand against the work of Satan and bring spiritual freedom into the lives of these believers.

PRAY FOR YOURSELF

I crown You as the only King and God of my life. I submit to Your lordship. If I have allowed any spiritual force into my life other than You to guide, protect, or influence me, I renounce and remove it in Jesus' name. Be my only Lord and God.

CHAPTER TEN
OPPOSITION

Ministry in Thailand is usually slow and often frustrating. Yet opposition to the gospel is rarely confrontative or violent. In fact, opposition in Thai culture usually begins with friendly smiles, nods, and gentle words, although their true meaning is, "Move on. We don't want you here."

Ministering in an atmosphere of constant opposition is demanding. It calls for grit, determination, vision, prayer, and a lot of stubbornness. But another outstanding element has helped me overcome the most difficult of trials: supportive relationships with other believers.

The most common metaphor the writers of Scripture used to describe God's people is *family*. We are brothers and sisters in Jesus Christ. In the midst of opposition, we need the support, encouragement, help, and partnership of our spiritual family to survive and thrive in ministry.

I was a shy, quiet kid growing up. I didn't fit in, and it didn't help that my family was the only Pentecostal one in town. Holdingford, Minnesota, had two churches—both Catholic. In fact, the culture was so Catholic that every Ash Wednesday the school took several hours off to bus all the kids to one of the two churches to receive the ash cross smudge on their forehead. Two other kids and I sat in the empty classroom while they were gone. But it was the dancing segment of our physical education class that really singled me out as different. The Assemblies of God believed dancing was sinful, so when our class learned square dancing, I presented a note from my parents requesting to be excused. I was the only one sitting on the side, and I felt like an oddball.

When I moved to Minneapolis to attend North Central University, I was used to being a loner. In fact, I preferred being alone. I was relieved to find out I would have no dorm roommate during my first year. I may have been the only person on the third floor without a roommate, and it made me happy.

Two doors down from me lived another freshman by the name of Kurt Jacobson. Kurt latched onto me within the first few days of school. He was lonely. He was from Kentucky, so Minnesota was a long way from home and family, and he desperately missed his girlfriend Andrea. Kurt was a talker, and I since I didn't say much, there was nothing stopping him from talking long and passionately about his eight brothers and sisters, his parents, his church, his Kentucky Wildcats, and most of all, Andrea. He was not brought up to hide intimate feelings as I was, and his transparency sometimes shocked me as he described how much he loved and missed Andrea. At times I tried to figure out ways to cut short those uncomfortable (to me) conversations, but I was too polite and shy to let him know I had heard enough.

Eventually Kurt changed my life. We ended up being together a lot during that first year at school. We both loved sports, so we played basketball and tennis together. We both got hired at a sheet metal shop near NCU, so besides studying together, we worked together every day too. Between our freshman and sophomore years, I took flying lessons at a local airport. One evening after my lesson, as I was backing my 1972 Vega out of its parking space, one wheel turned sideways. A tie rod dropped out of its socket, leaving me with no steering in the right wheel. I called Kurt. Immediately he dropped what he was doing, grabbed his tools, picked up a new tie rod end at the local auto parts store, and drove 17 miles to the airport to help me. We worked on the car well into the night, and that event triggered a change inside of me. I fully embraced—finally—the value of our friendship.

Kurt taught me how to be a true friend in many ways, but the real revelation was realizing God designed me to *need* a friend and to *be* a friend. His Great Commandment is to love God and love people. As a follower of Christ, I am obligated to relate to people, and He blesses me when I do (Psalm 133:3).

The lesson I learned about relationships was not earth-shattering, but when I began ministering in Thailand's spiritually hostile environment, my need for the strength and support of my brothers and sisters in Christ was magnified. We need one another. God designed us that way, and He is pleased when we operate in unity.

TOWN HALL OPPOSITION

Approximately two years into our weekly Bible studies in Ban Pong, we decided to start an after-school hangout center for kids. Our plan was to build friendships with the neighborhood kids and families by offering a fun place to play, free tutoring, English classes, music lessons, and other services. We rented a house with a big front yard just a block from the school and began to remodel it for our purposes. We took walls down to create a big room. We removed trees and bushes and leveled out the front yard to make a play area that included a basketball hoop and volleyball net. We painted the house inside and out. Within a few weeks, it was starting to look like a proper center for kids.

We were starting to fix up the walls surrounding the property when we received a notice from the township committee. They were calling an emergency town meeting and our after-school center (soon to be called Hosea Center) was the sole agenda item. We received less than a day's notice for this meeting.

While preparing for the meeting, I was thinking it could present a great opportunity to introduce ourselves to the people, tell them about our nonprofit Venture Foundation, and fill them in on the potential benefits and value the foundation would bring to Ban Pong and their children. I prepared a one-page summary that included our objectives: education, health, ethics, disaster relief, and teaching English.

Two others from Hosea Center accompanied me to the town hall: Pat, the host of the weekly house church in town, and Doi, a young Thai believer who I had been discipling for the past few years. We hired Doi as Hosea Center's director, and he moved into the center to be as closely connected to the village as possible. When we entered the meeting room, I was shocked to see it jammed full. At least 100 people were present, and there weren't enough chairs, so many people were standing along the walls. The head monk of the town's Buddhist temple was sitting next to the council members, and several other saffron-clad monks sat next to him. I later found out the abbot was behind this meeting. The atmosphere was tense.

Pat, Doi, and I sat off to one side. The Ban Pong township chairman opened the meeting by asking me what we were planning to do in their village. We distributed the pages I had prepared, and Doi briefly summarized our five objectives.

After a few moments of silence, one of the influential townsmen stood up. He went through the five objectives one by one. They didn't need our help with education, because they had a good school. They didn't need our help with health, because they had a clinic. They didn't need our help with ethics, because they had a temple. They didn't need our help with disasters, because they had a township seat. They could use help with English, but we didn't need to rent a building in their neighborhood to do that. We could set up somewhere else and commute to their school to teach English. They didn't want us living in their village.

When he finished talking, the crowd applauded. Several others took turns standing to say they did not want the influence of foreigners in their town, and each time there was a verbal assent to their comments. One person accused us of trying to convert the village to Christianity and commented that they were perfectly fine following Buddhism. I was glad they didn't ask me directly if that was our goal. The chairman summarized the meeting by saying he was sorry, but the town did not need or want us in the village.

How should I respond? I felt a strong urge to defend myself and Hosea Center. As a government-recognized foundation, we had a legal right to rent property and carry out our legal objectives wherever we so desired. The one thing that could legally prevent this was a clause that said we could not cause disruption in the village. I wanted to tell them we had a legal right to be there, and they were the ones causing disruption. But the Holy Spirit helped me bite my tongue, stand to my feet, smile, give them a big *wai*, thank them for the meeting, and walk out with Pat and Doi following me.

The three of us slowly returned to the center. The rejection stung. The whole village had conspired against us. Not a single person had spoken in our favor. We were upset. We had put a lot of planning, money, and work into the center, and now we were told to get out. I wondered what would happen if we ignored their decision. Could they win a court case against us if it came down to that? We desperately needed the guidance of the Holy Spirit.

Back at Hosea Center, we sat in a circle in the big room. I led in prayer, asking God to show us how to respond. We were all convinced God had orchestrated the house church at Pat's home. We believed God had birthed the idea of an after-school center and opened the door to rent the house we were renovating. We were confident God had plans for Ban Pong. But the door seemed to be closing fast.

I decided to place the decision in Pat and Doi's hands. I told them I thought we had a legal right to be there, and I was willing to fight the town hall decision. We all knew fighting would not endear us to the village and could provoke violence against us and our property. Since I did not live in the village and they did, they would bear the brunt of any reprisals leveled against us. If they were willing to take these risks, I was willing to stand with them and fight whatever legal battles were necessary.

Pat answered immediately. "We should stay," she said. "I don't care what they try to do to us. God led us to start this center, and we must do it."

Without hesitation, Doi concurred. Then he told an amazing story. When he was an adolescent, two Christian women rented a house next to his home village in a remote area near the border of Laos. The villagers learned they were Christians and tried to kick them out. When the women refused to leave, the villagers mistreated them, cursed them, and threw rocks at their house, damaging their roof tiles. The women persevered through the persecution. After six or seven years, the village finally began to accept them, and some began attending the house church they were trying to start. One of the women offered English classes, and Doi studied with her as a teenager. These two women taught Doi about Jesus, and through their influence, he became a strong believer.

"We should stay," Doi said. "The village will be mad at us and may persecute us for six or seven years, but eventually they will accept us just like the two women in my village. Then we will be free to share Jesus with them and their children."

Wow! God had prepared Doi for this situation many years before! Both he and Pat were ready to face anything the village could throw at them.

Indeed, the village opposed us, but surprisingly, not for long. When they saw we didn't move out, they prepared a petition against us and acquired the signatures of most of the village. We ignored their petition. At first they refused to allow their kids to come to the center, but that didn't last long.

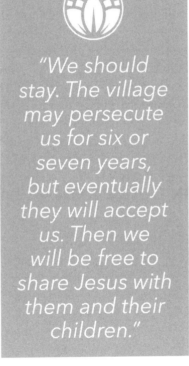

"We should stay. The village may persecute us for six or seven years, but eventually they will accept us. Then we will be free to share Jesus with them and their children."

Within one year the center was filled with kids playing games, learning English, studying piano, getting tutored, and hanging out.

Within two years the first group of believers emerged as five high-school kids gave their lives to Jesus. One of them, Aung, eventually became the director of the center. Today my oldest daughter Krista and her family serve as missionaries in Chiang Mai, and one of their responsibilities is to oversee Hosea Center, which continues to represent Jesus in Ban Pong.

God's planning is amazing. He prepared Doi for the challenges we faced by exposing him to an almost identical situation as a teenager. God prepared the hearts of Doi, Pat, and me to embolden each other to defy the will of the town meeting. He prepared Aung to grow as a believer and return to her home village as the director of the center. He prepared Krista and her family to return to Thailand to continue the work at Hosea Center. None of this happened because of the work of one person. We all needed each other to accomplish the task.

I started this chapter by saying that ministry in Thailand is usually slow and often frustrating. It cannot and will not be accomplished by lone rangers. We desperately need each other and must be intentional about building, cultivating, and maintaining unified relationships with coworkers. I love reading Paul's list of colleagues in Romans 16, where he mentions at least 37 people who were significant partners in his ministry. Paul's Kingdom accomplishments came about through a team approach. He needed other people, and so do we.

IN-OUT-UP-DOWN

God loves unity among Christians. He loves it so much that He commands blessings to fall wherever unity exists (Psalm 133:3). I have become radically committed to building and strengthening harmonious relationships with my family in Christ. Unity with my spiritual brothers and sisters is critical to success in ministry. Several events throughout the course of our ministry in Thailand highlight the need for and benefits of unity. These benefits are all-encompassing and four-dimensional: inward, outward, upward, and downward.

INWARD BENEFITS

During our first term in Thailand, Mary (not her real name), a college graduate in her 20s, joined the Peace

Corps and committed two years of her life to help Thai farmers improve their agricultural methods. Her assigned city was Chiang Kham, located some three hours northeast of our home in Chiang Mai. At the time, the only Americans living in Chiang Kham were our missionary friends, John and Jenny Goddard.

Beloved, I urge you as sojourners and exiles.
(1 Peter 2:11)

Our citizenship is in heaven, and from it we await a Savior, the Lord Jesus Christ.
(Philippians 3:20)

Mary's first few days in Chiang Kham were traumatic. She was 8000 miles from home. The weather was extremely hot and humid, and no one used air conditioners. The food was unbearably spicy. She couldn't speak Thai, and very few people spoke English. She struggled to understand every word from those who tried to speak English. Nothing was familiar or comfortable. She missed everything about America, especially her family.

Just days after her arrival, Mary decided she couldn't take it anymore. She dialed her mother from a sidewalk telephone booth (this was before cell phones existed) and cried as she told her of her decision to return to the U.S. In the middle of her conversation, Mary saw my friend John walking down the sidewalk on the opposite side of the street. John is a big man with red hair and a fair complexion. It was obvious this man was not Thai.

Mary shouted to her mom that she had to go, slammed the phone down, and ran across the street towards John. As she approached, she gushed, "Do you speak English?"

"I sure do, ma'am," John replied.

Mary had no words. She hugged John and cried, overcome with relief to meet someone who understood and identified with her.

John invited Mary to their home for dinner, where Jenny served hamburgers, baked beans, and apple pie. They talked late into the evening before John brought her back to the guest house where she was staying. From that time on, Mary spent time with John and Jenny nearly every day. You guessed it: Mary was able to complete her two-year term in Chiang Kham, because someone understood her language and culture.

As believers we are aliens in this world, just like Mary was an alien in Chiang Kham. Our citizenship is in heaven. Our culture is biblical. Our brothers and sisters are fellow believers. The *inward benefit* of unity is that it gives us strength to survive in this foreign world. When we speak the language of faith with likeminded believers, we're encouraged. When we're in trouble, in need, lonely, or lost, we rely on each other for help. We "rejoice with those who rejoice, [and] weep with those who weep" (Romans 12:15). Without the unity of believers, we will not survive in this world; but in unity we will make it through this earthly assignment, just as Mary made it through hers.

> [I ask] that they may all be one, just as you, Father, are in me, and I in you, that they also may be in us, so that the world may believe that you have sent me.
> (John 17:21)

OUTWARD BENEFITS

During our first term in Thailand, we started a weekly small group Bible study for university students at our home. Among the attendees was a student named Jip. Strangely, Jip was not a Christian. She was the only Buddhist attending, and she came faithfully every week. We did very Christian things in the group. We worshiped. We prayed. We studied the Bible. It wasn't an evangelistic Bible study but focused on discipleship. I wondered why Jip kept coming back.

One evening after the study, I took Jip aside and asked her what attracted her to our weekly meetings. Why did she, a professing Buddhist, faithfully attend our Christian Bible studies? Her response made Jesus' words in John 17:21 leap to life. She thought for a moment, and then explained that whenever she went out with her non-Christian friends, she had to guard herself against being taken advantage of. But it wasn't like that at our Bible studies. There she felt "warm and safe."

The atmosphere of Christian unity is warm and safe. When non-believers experience it, they know it is special. It is distinct from the world's atmosphere. The benefit of unity extends *outward* into the unbelieving world as a witness that Jesus is real. That's what Jesus prayed in John 17:21. He knew evangelism is easy when we live in harmonious relationship with each other. The world is attracted to an atmosphere that is warm and safe.

It wasn't long after my conversation with Jip that she decided to place her faith in Christ. A unified church is a growing church!

UPWARD BENEFITS

One day while reading Jesus' promise in Matthew 18:19, a question came to my mind. Why did Jesus promise that when *two* people agree in prayer the heavenly Father will hear and answer their prayer? His promise begs the question, doesn't the Father hear and answer single-person prayers? Of course, God hears the prayers of individuals. Jesus' other instructions on prayer do not mention group prayers, so we know this is not a required approach. However, Matthew recalls Jesus making the distinct point that when two people pray together about something, God hears and answers.

The *upward benefit* of unified relationships is that God favors the kind of prayer that happens jointly. Prayers are more effective and God's miracle-working power is more

> Again I say to you, if two of you agree on earth about anything they ask, it will be done for them by my Father in heaven.
> (Matthew 18:19)
>
> Behold, how good and pleasant it is when brothers dwell in unity!... For there the Lord has commanded the blessing, life forevermore.
> (Psalm 133:1,3)

available when people agree together in prayer. God likes unity. Psalm 133 tells us God commands blessings when His people operate in unity.

Ministry among Buddhists is extremely challenging. The constant flow of difficult situations demands constant prayer. I need brothers and sisters in Christ to agree with me in prayer. There are times when I realize I have been laboring alone in prayer over a situation that isn't getting better, and I realize I need to put into practice the multi-person prayer principle. I must ask someone to pray for me and with me. Many times throughout years of ministry in Thailand, I have experienced the positive impact of prayers for me. I don't want to labor alone, and I don't have to labor alone, because people are praying for me.

If you have been praying alone over problems without seeing answers, go to a friend and ask them to pray along with you. God wants us to come to Him *together*. He makes His power more readily available when we function in unity with other believers.

DOWNWARD BENEFITS

It is not illegal to convert to Christianity in Thailand, but when people living in small villages do so, it is extremely difficult for them and the entire village. Rural Thai villages are tightly knit. Everyone knows what is going on in everyone else's life. Their culture is known as "collective," meaning the group is more important than the individual.

Everyone is expected to prioritize the needs of the village over their own needs. When an individual doesn't conform or does something that is perceived to be detrimental to the village, the entire village rises up against him or her to regain collective harmony. That's what happened in Ban Pong when Hosea Center started. The village perceived it to be a strange, nonconformist threat to their harmony. There were also spiritual factors involved, but the opposition by village leaders was a typical collective culture response.

Though a man might prevail against one who is alone, two will withstand him—a threefold cord is not quickly broken. (Ecclesiastes 4:12)

Five of you shall chase a hundred, and a hundred of you shall chase ten thousand. (Leviticus 26:8)

A family in the rural village of Bo Sali became believers through the witness of relatives. The village was concerned this would disrupt the harmony of their village. The family would no longer contribute to the local temple or attend Buddhist ceremonies conducted there. They would not participate in spirit-appeasing ceremonies. Besides that, the village feared the family would invoke retribution and curses from spirits who were unhappy with their decision. So the village conducted a special meeting and ordered the family to reverse their decision. They refused.

Once again the village called a special meeting. This time they laid down an ultimatum. If the family did not renounce their Christian faith, their electricity and water would be cut off. The family refused to back down, and as promised, their utilities were cut.

When Christians in a nearby village heard the news, they began visiting the family regularly, bringing encouragement, prayer, and water along with them. The family not only weathered the storm but prospered. Their neighbors were so impressed with the care and love they received from other Christians, they decided to become Christians as well. The village had no choice but to restore their electricity and water.

The *downward benefit* of unity refers to believers' strength in the face of attack from the enemy of our soul, Satan. God has given us a powerful weapon to counteract these attacks. Unity can carry us through as the body of Christ surrounds us. The catch is, we must acknowledge our need to live in relationship with other believers and cultivate relationships so we are in the position to help or be helped in times of need. We need each other!

Perhaps you are reeling under enemy attack. Pursue unity. Some people tend to hide their pain from other believers during times of need, maybe because of shame. Job felt shame amid the incredible losses he incurred, although he knew the disasters were not his fault (Job 10:15). Facing challenges does not mean you deserve them. Job was the most righteous man on the earth (1:8), and he didn't deserve the disasters he suffered. You don't deserve the attack you're under either. Don't try to bear your burden alone and ashamed. Unified, loving relationships are a precious gift that will give you victory over the enemy.

SPIRITUAL INSIGHTS & PRAYERS

God loves unity. He made people to relate to Him and each other. We are incomplete without other people in our lives. Believers benefit from close relationships with other believers. When opposition arises, relational unity provides support, strength, wisdom, provision, and most of all, a special blessing commanded by God (Psalm 133:3). Unity yields inward, outward, upward, and downward benefits. If you are in need, seek out a like-minded believer to help you work and pray it through.

PRAY FOR BUDDHISTS

I pray for unity among Buddhist-background believers. May they encourage and strengthen each other by their love. Draw others to You as their unity is obvious to the world. Hear and answer their unified prayers. May their unity give them victory over the evil one and the challenges they face today.

PRAY FOR MISSIONARIES

I pray for unity between missionaries who work in Buddhist contexts. Help them forgive, love, and support one another and live as Your examples before the Buddhists they came to reach. Unify pastors and Christian leaders in the Buddhist world, that they will "[submit] to one another out of reverence for Christ" (Ephesians 5:21).

PRAY FOR YOURSELF

Help me foster unity in my church and with other believers. Help me encourage and build them up rather than tear them down, forgive them when they hurt me, and love them as Your Word commands (1 John 4:7–8). May the unity I have with my Christian friends demonstrate to unbelievers that You are real.

CONCLUSION
JOIN THE BATTLE

Since 2013 Change The Map has produced a monthly prayer guide that shares a testimony or lesson from the Buddhist world and lists weekly prayer requests to guide those who take up the challenge to pray for Buddhists. Several missionaries have now joined me in donating their time to write, edit, format, and publish these prayer guides as emails and social media posts.

As of the writing of this book, Change The Map has roughly 4500 subscribers or followers of the monthly prayer guide for Buddhists. My goal is to grow that number to 25,000 in my lifetime.

Yesterday my dad was laid to rest at Minnesota State Veterans Cemetery at Fort Ripley. Because of COVID-19 travel restrictions, I couldn't leave Thailand to attend the ceremony. Well, I could have left, but I wouldn't have been able to return. My three brothers and sister helped my mom through the difficult days since Dad died late on Christmas Day. I am dedicating this book to Dad, because he vicariously touched the lives of untold thousands in the Buddhist world.

Dad was born to simple immigrant farmers in central Minnesota. He was a multi-skilled craftsman throughout his life and made a good living through his HVAC business. He felled trees and sawed them into boards with his lumber mill. He drilled wells. He welded all sorts of metals. He was the neighborhood fix-it man and usually refused to accept payment for his work. He built sheet metal ductwork. He fashioned all kinds of things on his metal lathe. He tapped maple trees and boiled the sap into syrup. He hunted and fished and loved the outdoors. Best of all, he and Mom raised five kids to love and serve Jesus.

Dad's life impacted me. As a young child, I saw something I'll never forget. It was a tear coming out of Dad's eye one Sunday night at the altar of our church. I had never seen Dad cry or show much emotion of any kind before that. That little tear told me Dad was wholly and completely committed to following Jesus.

Dad probably didn't think he impacted Thailand and the Buddhist world, but he did. Without Dad, I wouldn't be a missionary in Thailand. I feel the same way about those who are praying for Buddhists. You don't understand how significant your prayers are. Just as the staff in Moses' hand was more powerful than the swords in the soldiers' hands on the battlefield against the Amalekites, so your prayers for Buddhists are the most powerful weapon that can be wielded in the battle for their souls.

Will you join this battle to change the map of the Buddhist world? When thousands cry out to God faithfully in prayer, doors of salvation will open, despite having been firmly closed since the time of Christ. I pray that this book will inspire you to join the prayer adventure now at www.ctm.world or by following Change The Map on Facebook, Twitter, or Instagram. May God's power be unleashed through you to change the spiritual map of the Buddhist world!

MAP OF WORLD BUDDHISTS

THERAVADA BUDDHISM

TIBETAN BUDDHISM

MAHAYANA BUDDHISM

Most of the world's Buddhists live in seven nations: China, Japan, Thailand, Vietnam, Myanmar, Cambodia, and Sri Lanka. Counting the worldwide Buddhist population is challenging, because wherever it has spread, Buddhism tends to syncretize its practices to look like the existing local religion. For example, Shintoism preceded Buddhism in Japan, but over time the two practices have been described as "functionally inseparable."[20] A recent study revealed that 85 percent of Japanese people follow Shintoism while at the same time 75 percent follow Buddhism.[21] Similar crossover characteristics exist in China and other Eastern nations. Most leading missiologists working among Buddhists estimate the number of Buddhist followers to be near 1 billion. It is the world's fourth-largest religion, following Christianity, Islam, and Hinduism.

Three major branches of Buddhism developed in the regions indicated on the map on page 165. Each branch has distinctive practices and beliefs, but all ascribe to some aspect of the teachings of Siddhartha Gautama, the first Buddha, including the Four Noble Truths as described on page 61. For more information, visit www.ctm.world.

20 https://en.wikipedia.org/wiki/Shinto, accessed 2/17/2021.
21 http://factsanddetails.com/japan/cat16/sub182/item592.html, accessed 2/17/2020.

APPENDIX B

SPIRITUAL INSIGHTS AND PRAYERS

INTRODUCTION: CHANGE THE MAP

Missiologists say there are approximately 1 billion Buddhists in the world. They are eternally lost without Jesus' saving grace. Missionaries work hard, but they cannot win the Buddhist world to Jesus alone. Just as Moses' staff ensured Israel's triumph over the Amalekites, the staff of intercession is our key to victory. You hold the staff. Your prayers are needed to Change The Map.

CHAPTER ONE: THE DOME

When you follow God's leading to the best of your ability—no matter where you live, work, or travel—you dwell under the dome of God's protection. If God protected me and my family through the intense spiritual darkness of the guru house, He will protect you through your trials. When spiritual forces attack from every side, you can be confident that His mighty power living inside you is greater than the power of evil that surrounds you on the outside.

CHAPTER TWO: PROPERTY SPIRITS

Idols are powerless until people worship them. This principle is true whether the idol is a figurine, a person, or even a concept. When people worship anything besides God, they expose themselves to the risk of demonic activity. Thai Buddhists and the majority of Eastern Buddhists believe idols and spirits are real and powerful. They worship them openly, resulting in an atmosphere charged with spiritual activity. Our prayers are needed to release people from the control of demons and open their spiritual ears to hear the Holy Spirit calling out to them through the darkness.

CHAPTER THREE: THE SECRET POWER OF WORSHIP

God created humankind as His highest creation and as spiritual beings who possess the ability to communicate with the unseen spiritual realm. Worship is the primary language in that realm, whether we are communicating with the Creator or with the things He created. As Buddhists worship created things, their enslavement to demonic powers deepens. As believers worship God, their relationship with Him grows stronger.

CHAPTER FOUR: THE GOSPEL DOESN'T MAKE SENSE

Because of their worldview, Buddhists may misunderstand the precious gospel message. They may view God as evil, love as weak, the cross as bad karma, and eternal life as a trap. Communicating the gospel to Buddhists in an understandable way requires cultural insight and, more importantly, divine inspiration. God's plan of salvation surpasses cultural barriers, and those who effectively communicate the message need Holy Spirit guidance.

CHAPTER FIVE: GOD IS GOOD!

Buddhists teach that suffering and existence are inseparable. According to this reasoning, if a creator god exists, he is evil, because he created an existence of suffering. The concept of a good God is foreign to Thai Buddhists. To complicate this challenge, the Old Testament sacrificial system appears offensive to Buddhists who are taught that killing animals is murder, and it reinforces the notion that God is evil. However, Genesis 1-4 explains the origin of suffering and depicts God as completely good and abundantly merciful. Despite the reality of suffering in the world, God is good and desires good things for all people.

CHAPTER SIX: BELIEVERS OR SEEKERS?

The Eastern Buddhist worldview is oceans apart from the biblical worldview. It can take many years for a Buddhist to understand what salvation and lordship mean. Rather than pressing them to pray the "sinner's prayer" when they don't fully comprehend the meaning of salvation, we invite them to pray the "seeker's prayer," pledging to search for God until they find Him. Then we faithfully disciple them until they voluntarily and knowingly place their faith in Jesus.

CHAPTER SEVEN: BARRIERS

When leading someone to a saving knowledge of Jesus, there is often one major stumbling block keeping him or her from taking a step of faith. For Sai it was her belief in her father's ghost. For Pat it was her funeral. Often we do not know what the barrier is, and we must rely on the Holy Spirit to reveal it. When we know what it is, we must pray until God reveals the solution. God knows how to remove barriers and release people to welcome Jesus into their lives.

CHAPTER EIGHT: BAPTISM OR MONKHOOD?

Regardless of one's religious background, discipleship is crucial for new believers, especially Buddhist-background believers. Effective discipleship happens in the context of a personal relationship between a disciple and a discipler who are interacting together under the Holy Spirit's supernatural guidance. This discipleship process is not complete until reproduction takes place.

CHAPTER NINE: A DAUGHTER OF WITCH DOCTORS

Spiritual freedom can be challenging for believers with histories of demonic involvement. They must be willing to renounce all ungodly spiritual alliances and remove related objects—physical, conceptual, or spiritual—from their lives to maintain freedom from demonic influence. Most Eastern Buddhists live in cultures where demonic involvement is common. New believers coming out of those cultures need our prayers for their spiritual freedom.

CHAPTER TEN: OPPOSITION

God loves unity. He made people to relate to Him and each other. We are incomplete without other people in our lives. Believers benefit from close relationships with other believers. When opposition arises, relational unity provides support, strength, wisdom, provision, and most of all, a special blessing commanded by God (Psalm 133:3). Unity yields inward, outward, upward, and downward benefits. If you are in need, seek out a like-minded believer to help you work and pray it through.

PRAYERS FOR BUDDHISTS

I pray for the 1 billion Buddhists in the world who need You as Savior and Lord. Please reveal Yourself to them, communicate Your love to them, open their minds to Your truth, and open their hearts to receive You.

I pray for Buddhist-background believers throughout the world who are living in atmospheres of pervasive spiritual darkness. God, please cover them with a dome of spiritual protection. Instead of giving in to fear or succumbing to the evil that surrounds them, may they be strong and courageous under Your wings (Psalm 91).

I pray for Buddhists throughout the world who live in atmospheres of intense spiritual darkness. May their eyes be drawn to the light. May their ears be open to the truth. May their minds comprehend the gospel. May their spirits be receptive to Jesus' saving power so they can say, "He has delivered us from the domain of darkness and transferred us to the kingdom of his beloved Son" (Colossians 1:13).

As Buddhists bow before idols, open their minds to the revelation they are slipping deeper and deeper underneath the influence of dark powers that control them rather than giving them freedom. May they recognize that idol worship is enslaving them spiritually and have courage to stop honoring idols and begin to pursue You.

I pray for Buddhists who misunderstand the gospel because of their worldview. Holy Spirit, please reveal God's amazing love for them and the wonder of Jesus' atoning work on the cross. May the gospel message make sense to them, and may they place their faith in You.

I pray for Buddhists who believe that if You exist, You must be evil, because You created a world of suffering. May they recognize Your goodness and turn to You for salvation.

I pray thousands of Buddhists will grow curious about the Christian message. May they find a Bible or Christian literature that will attract their interest. Send believers to guide them to become seekers and help them pursue the knowledge of You.

I pray for Buddhists who are interested in following Christ but have barriers preventing them from taking that step. God, reveal the barriers and make a way to overcome them and follow You.

I pray Buddhist-background seekers and new believers will become strongly connected with mature believers who will disciple them patiently and accurately for as long as it takes to become reproducing disciplers. Through discipleship, the Scriptures, and Your guidance, transform them into strong, solid, unshakable followers of Jesus Christ.

I pray for Buddhist-background believers who were saved from demonic involvement. May they be bold to renounce and remove all demonic influences. Let Your dome of protection cover them and provide complete spiritual freedom.

I pray for unity among Buddhist-background believers. May they encourage and strengthen each other by their love. Draw others to You as their unity is obvious to the world around them. Hear their unified prayers and answer them powerfully. May their unity give them victory over the evil one and the many challenges they are facing today.

PRAYERS FOR MISSIONARIES

I lift up the staff of intercession on behalf of missionaries and Christian workers living and ministering in the Buddhist world. Cover them with anointing, fill them with faith and boldness, and let Your provision and protection rest on them and their families.

Holy Spirit, please cover missionaries and Christian workers with Your dome of protection wherever they are. I pray 1 John 4:4 over them.

I pray for strength for missionaries and Christian workers who are ministering in spiritually dark places. I prayerfully support them in spiritual warfare, according to Ephesians 6:10-12.

I pray missionaries and Christian workers who live among idol worshippers will worship God with increasing intensity and that God's presence within and around them will increase so that everyone around them will sense the powerful presence of the Holy Spirit.

I pray missionaries and Christian workers will communicate the gospel message to Buddhists in a culturally contextualized and divinely inspired way, so they will understand its true meaning. Fill believers with wisdom and anointing as they witness. I pray Colossians 4:3–4 over them.

I pray missionaries and Christian workers will operate in the gifts of words of wisdom and knowledge as they communicate the gospel to Buddhists. Inspire them with insightful, effective ways to teach about Your goodness despite the existence of suffering.

I pray missionaries and Christian workers will have divine appointments with Buddhists who are ready to become seekers. Prepare them to lead these seekers to search until they find You as Savior and Lord.

I pray missionaries and Christian workers will be sensitive to Your voice to recognize key barriers that hold Buddhists back from salvation. Give them wisdom and anointing to help Buddhists overcome those barriers and follow You.

I pray missionaries and Christian workers will be eager and prepared to disciple Buddhist-background seekers and new believers. Anoint them to exercise the gifts of the Holy Spirit as they guide their disciples into maturity in Christ.

I pray for a special anointing to fall on missionaries and Christian workers to discern and rebuke demonic influences at work in the lives of new Buddhist-background believers. Equip them spiritually, and make them ready to stand against the work of Satan and bring spiritual freedom into the lives of these believers.

I pray for unity between missionaries who work in Buddhist contexts. Help them forgive, love, and support one another and live as Your examples before the Buddhists they came to reach. Unify pastors and Christian leaders in the Buddhist world, that they will "[submit] to one another out of reverence for Christ" (Ephesians 5:21).

PRAYERS FOR YOURSELF

Through the battles in my life, I pray You will give me faith and courage to place my trust in the staff more than the sword. Burden my heart to pray for Buddhists with Your love and concern. Use me as part of the army of intercessors who will change the map for Your sake.

Wherever I go and whatever I do, let the indwelling presence of the Holy Spirit surround and protect me. According to Psalm 91, I place my trust in You.

I pray that I would never worship anyone or anything besides You, according to Exodus 20:3. You are the Lord of my life, my thoughts, my decisions, my possessions, my relationships, my past, my present, and my future.

I pray my worship of You will grow in consistency. As I worship, fill me and my family with Your presence in increasing measure. May the presence of the Holy Spirit in me become more and more obvious to people around me.

I pray for courage to build friendships with Buddhists. Give me opportunities to share Jesus with them, and teach me to be sensitive to their worldview and hear and follow the Holy Spirit's voice.

I pray when I am going through times of suffering and challenge, I will turn to You, sense Your comfort, and be reassured of Your goodness. When people around me suffer, show me how to encourage them and reassure them of Your goodness.

I pray for the opportunity to meet Buddhist seekers who are curious about You. Help me be willing to spend time with them, show them who You are, lead them to trust in You, and guide them into growing as true followers.

I pray for my relatives and friends who are not believers. Reveal the barriers that stand in the way of their salvation. I confront those barriers in Your name and ask for wisdom to know what to do to help my loved ones overcome them and receive salvation.

Holy Spirit, use me to disciple someone. May my life and words encourage, strengthen, guide, and mentor younger believers to love You with all their hearts, souls, minds, and strength.

I crown You as the only King and God of my life. I submit to Your lordship. If I have allowed any spiritual force into my life other than You to guide, protect, or influence me, I renounce and remove it in Jesus' name. Be my only Lord and God.

Help me foster unity in my church and with other believers. Help me encourage and build them up rather than tear them down. Help me forgive them when they hurt me. Help me love them as Your Word commands (1 John 4:7-8). May the unity I have with my Christian friends demonstrate to unbelievers that You are real.

ACKNOWLEDGMENTS

I couldn't have written this book without my wife Janie. Thank you for your patience, love, and support throughout this project.

Bishop Rick Thomas—thank you for birthing the idea of a *Change the Map* book. You started this!

Jeff Dove—thank you for faithfully pressing me to keep writing this book. It took three years to get me going, but your encouragement worked!

Randy Young—thank you for keeping me accountable to write every Monday and Friday. Your accountability kept me on task.

Greg Mundis and Jeff Hartensveld, my AGWM leaders—thank you for supporting this project.

Lauren Becker—thank you for your excellent feedback and edits on every chapter in this book.

Alan Johnson, Gary Martindale, and Jim Bradford— thank you for your advice, edits, and encouragement.

Krista Smith, my oldest daughter—thank you for transcribing one of my sermons to give me a head start on several of these topics.

Sharon Rose, my sister-in-law and an accomplished author—thank you for inspiring me to step out and start writing.

Nick Serban and Aaron Smith—thank you for creating the cover and the Appendix A map.

Josh, Lauren, Jacob, and Marcia—thank you for your hard work with CTM every week.